CARP

Rob Maylin

Beekay Publishers

Other angling titles by Beekay Publishers

Coarse

Carp Fever by Kevin Maddocks
The Art of Pole Fishing by Dickie Carr
Pike Fishing in the 80's by Neville Fickling
Basic Carp Fishing by Peter Mohan
Modern Specimen Hunting by Jim Gibbinson
Top Ten — tactics for the major species from ten leading anglers
Edited by Bruce Vaughan
Redmire Pool by Kevin Clifford & Len Arbery
Tactics for Big Pike by Bill Chillingworth
In Pursuit of Carp & Catfish by Kevin Maddocks
Cypry The Carp by Peter Mohan
The Beekay Guide to 450 Carp Waters
Jim Davidson Gets Hooked by Jim Davidson
In Pursuit of Predatory Fish by Neville Fickling
Tiger Bay by Rob Maylin
Understanding Barbel by Fred Crouch
Big-Water Carp by Jim Gibbinson
Mega-Pike by Eddie Turner

Sea

Boat Fishing at Sea by Phill Williams & Brian Douglas
Long Range Casting & Fishing Techniques by Paul Kerry
Cod Fishing by John Rawle
Uptide & Boatcasting by Bob Cox

Game

The Colour Guide to Fly Tying by Kevin Hyatt
Robson's Guide to Stillwater Trout Flies by Kenneth Robson
Dressed to Kill by Bob Carnill & Kenneth Robson

First published in 1990 by
BEEKAY PUBLISHERS
WITHY POOL, BEDFORD ROAD,
HENLOW CAMP, BEDS. SG16 6EA
© Beekay Publishers 1990
ISBN 0 947674 31 4

Typeset by BP Integraphics Ltd., Bath, Avon
Printed in Great Britain at The Bath Press, Avon

Contents

Photographs by the author and friends
Drawings by Len Gurd

Introduction

In the New Year I found myself fishing with one of the most well known carp anglers in the country. In all the years I had been fishing we had never found ourselves fishing alongside each other which in today's world of big fish anglers is quite incredible. Of course I knew Kevin Maddocks well, as over the years we have spent quite a lot of time together through the Carp Anglers Association and the publication of my first book *Tiger Bay*, but we had never 'crossed lines', to coin a phrase.

Kevin was in the middle of producing a series of instructive reference books with a view towards successful anglers in all fields of the sport which I am sure you will see in the list of titles available in this series. I think it was I who first mentioned the carp book with no intention on my behalf that I would actually end up writing the thing. I had pre-empted a question that he had been waiting for the right moment to ask. Would I be interested in taking on the task? A text book, a reference book bang up-to-date, the waters, the methods, basically how to catch big carp, or how I catch them anyway.

Knowing my true style of writing which I would describe as 'relaxed' story telling this would be something entirely different from my two previous books. That's okay, I thought perhaps it would be a bit of a change. I was already working on the follow-up to *Fox Pool* which hopefully will be around at the end of 1991, but in the meantime I quite fancied trying to give some technical advice. So I sat down and worked out a few guidelines, choosing the right water with very big carp in mind, field work and preparation, pre-baiting, plumbing, location and rigs. Rigs I had already done before and you can't really change already established rigs so I've done a complete rig book of my own rigs if you like; bait, an up-to-date look at mixes, bait soaks and particles, floater fishing and finally comparisons between summer and winter fishing. So that was the way the book was going to be written and I felt I could probably do it, so I agreed. So that's what you are buying here, not a book along the lines of *Tiger Bay* or *Fox Pool* but a reference book, a book that you will be able to pick up time and time again when you come across certain problems on the water you are fishing.

These are my views, my conclusions, and it's certainly not the only way to do it. On the other hand I seem to catch more than my share of big fish so I must be doing something right if only fishing the right waters. I would hope that everyone might glean some amount of knowledge from this book and if you do then it's all been worthwhile.

Choosing The Right Water

When considering fishing exclusively for very big fish, by which I mean carp in excess of thirty pounds in weight, there are two very different types of approach. You can either fish for known big fish or you can tackle the unknown and pioneer a new water where little or no knowledge of recent carp captures are known. This book will deal mainly with my approach to known big fish waters, something I have been practising for the past eight years. I will devote a small section to pioneering new waters but the subject is so diverse that a separate book could be written on that subject alone.

The obvious advantages of fishing for known big fish will soon become apparent as you get deeper into the book but this is not to say that fishing for known fish is better or worse than that of fishing for the unknown. It is of course the dream of every carp man to discover some quiet neglected pool absolutely jam packed with monsters, but the realists amongst you would soon admit that for most of us a dream is all it will ever be.

Fishing for known big fish also has its own interest. To know your opponent can bring an intimacy between you and the carp which can only exist with this type of fishing. You may find yourself cursing the fish one day for its wariness or its strength and holding it in your arms another day, your ambition achieved at last. So to those who scorn the angler's intent at catching the 'same old faces', I say give it a try before you knock it—you may find a few surprises.

Before I go on to describe my approach to big carp fishing let me first describe the type of waters that will form the basis on which we can work. There are now books available which spell out all the details of many big fish waters throughout the country, and it is not my intention to repeat all of that, so if you want directions buy the *Guide to 450 Carp Waters* published by Beekay, but I will mention some of the waters I have actually fished and some of the others which close friends have tackled.

First of all, there is Savay Lake; there cannot be many who will be reading this book who haven't heard of Savay, at Denham in Buckinghamshire.

This lake is sixty odd acres of mature gravel pit which offer both syndicate and day ticket fishing for those who wish to try their luck and don't be put off if you can't get into the syndicate, as excellent fishing can be obtained on the day ticket part of the fishery. It's certainly not easy though, and these carp have had almost everything chucked at them over the past twenty years, so don't expect a hatfull if you do give it a try. I say it's not easy, and for catching large numbers of carp it certainly isn't, but if it's the chance of a thirty pound plus fish Savay must give you the best chance considering the large head of fish in this class. Don't ask me how many thirties there are because I really don't know but between twenty to thirty is certainly on the cards, and there are no other waters in this country that I am aware of that have as many different big fish.

The largest fish so far taken from Savay is a well known big common, affectionately named Sally. Last time out she was 39lb, so could a forty be on the cards? Martin Locke was the fortunate angler to have caught her last. Another friend of mine, Steve Allcott, caught what is now the largest mirror in Savay while I was in the syndicate, a fish which is now around the 37lb mark. It is interesting to me that many of the thirty pound plus fish have maintained a steady weight over quite a few number of years. Very few seem to be breaking the 35lb mark, so I wonder if they have now levelled off or reached a peak for the diet they now exist on. I wonder if in the next couple of seasons the high fat bait soaks which seem to have contributed to a higher than normal growth rate on such waters as Darenth will be used at Savay to such an extent that the Savay fish jump in weight to a comparable degree to the Darenth fish. If they did we could well see the first water with multiple forty pound plus fish; mind blowing! Perhaps I'll put my neck on the line and bet it would be the three or four big 'Italians' in Savay that would be the biggest gainers in weight. They are certainly the ones with the biggest appetites that I came across while I was there.

Savay is only one of many large gravel pits in this area, the Colne Valley, and almost any pit you could care to mention in this chain contains very big carp. Harefield lake, John Stent's showpiece, is another excellent fishery situated on the other side of the road from Savay. There are quite a few 30lb plus fish, including a 30lb fully scaled mirror in immaculate condition. By the time this book comes out Harefield will have had an injection of even larger fish as one of William Boyer's other waters, Rodney Meadow, is due to be emptied and the fish split between Harefield and Farlows. Harefield will receive the big boys.

Although run as a syndicate it's far from impossible to get in. Dougal Gray is the man to ask, and you will find him in the Horse and Barge Public House, opposite the lake most evenings. He likes Fosters lager!

As to the exact stocks and assuming the Rodney fish go in you are probably looking at thirties quickly approaching double figures and if the weights continue to grow as they have been doing, well the mind boggles.

Those of you who have read either *Tiger Bay* or *Fox Pool* will have heard of Springwood, an excellent fishery, and extremely difficult to get into; I am afraid that most of us will just have to sit back and watch. However I will mention it as many of the things I will be covering later in the book were learnt when I fished this water. I would guess there could well be around twenty, thirty pound fish in the lake now, and about three of them look as if they might do the forty. I'll put my neck on the line again and say that I think the number of forties we will be fishing for in the 1990's will be three times what we had fished for in the 1980's. The only trouble is there will be ten times as many people fishing for them!

Whereas those first three waters might be deemed as a bit difficult to join, the other waters I am about to mention are either day ticket or open club membership. Waveney Valley lakes at Wortwell in Norfolk is a day ticket fishery which consists of about a dozen smallish lakes, at least three of which contain thirty pound plus fish. These are lakes C, D and E. The lakes are allocated individual letters and if you wish to visit the fishery you will soon be put right as to which lake is which. Almost every carp fisherman I have met on the hard southern circuit waters have at one time or another fished at Waveney. It is a beautiful little place with excellent facilities and some good fish as well, probably half a dozen now around the thirty pound mark. This is where I caught my first thirty and I know many others who had equally good fortunes.

Darenth, Staines, Yateley and Wraysbury are all controlled by Leisure Sport Angling. They are managed by Jack Ashford, who has run these and Leisure Sport's other fisheries with great efficiency for many years from his office at Thorpe Park in Staines. Unfortunately the Staines fishery is now closed to angling and the many big fish have now been moved. Staines was a remarkable water which contained two different forty pound fish during its lifetime, though never more than one at any one time, plus another eight to ten thirties, many of which originated from Yeoveney lake which was also filled in for 'progress'! Perhaps these poor old fish will finally be allowed to settle once they are introduced to their new home.

The other three, Darenth, Yateley and Wraysbury, all contain very big fish and all have been well documented in the past. Of the three I feel Darenth has the potential to provide at least three new forties in the next couple of years which would, I feel, make it the premier water in the country. I haven't fished Darenth but I am informed that three different 38 lb plus fish came from Darenth Tip Lake in the 1989–90 season.

Yateley has at least two forties on the complex, which comprises about ten lakes, some of which have received little attention and some, such as the North, Car Park and Match Lake, which receive constant pressure. The Match Lake may be the one to watch this decade as the fish have been gradually climbing and are now into the thirties; because of the greater head of fish in this lake several could soon be very big.

Until recent years Wraysbury was a bit of a mystery water, and some say it still has its secrets. Peter Springate and Kenny Hodder did the business on there about two years ago. Fish in excess of 36lb are definitely in there. Forties—time will tell.

I think I've probably gone on enough about waters. Most people now have a water with fish around the thirty pound mark not too far from where they live, though it's catching them that's the trouble, and this is what I'd like to help you to do. So, this is what I would do when planning to fish a new water which I know contains a big fish. I must stress that this is only what I do—any conclusions I draw are based on my experiences, and I've been known to be wrong before and will be again, but at least I may be able to trigger some thoughts in your head which may put a couple of big fish on the bank for you.

Preparation

Before I actually begin to fish a new water I will always try to accumulate as much information about the place as possible. Sometimes this information is only a slight shove in the right direction such as someone showing you a few photos of fish he has actually taken from the water, but on more well known waters there will already be a great deal of information quite easily available. The weekly angling papers often carry reports of known fish. Carp Angling and Specialist big fish magazines will almost certainly have articles about known big fish waters, and of course books such as *Fox Pool* which have writers from a variety of waters can be invaluable.

It is essential to be sure that the fish you are going after actually exist in the water. We hear all too many stories of gigantic 'mythical' fish up and down the country, but I'm afraid I'm too much of a realist and have always been of the opinion that the biggest fish in the lake are only the biggest because they eat the most, so consequently they get caught, often more than the smaller fish in the lake, so unless I actually know whoever has claimed to have caught the fish or I see positive photographic proof, or I see it with my own eyes, I don't usually pay too much attention to gossip.

It may be possible to visit the water before you intend to fish it, either in or out of season. During the season a great deal can be learnt by watching the anglers already on the water. I don't mean by pestering everybody until they get the right hump with you, but a slow walk round every now and again, with a bit of careful observation as to where the consistent catchers are fishing and at what time of year. Most carp anglers are quite friendly sorts and without pushing too hard they can be all too willing to tell of their successes.

The close season can be a lot more useful providing you are allowed on the water. This is when I would take a really good look around the water. Armed with a decent set of polarised sun glasses and a plumbing rod I would try to discover as much about the carp's habitat as possible; you cannot possibly know too much about the topography of the lake bed. On many of these hard fished waters small clean areas of bottom can mean the difference between success and failure. Plumbing can be used in several different ways. The two I use most frequently are:

(1) Fixing the float at a measured distance above the lead, say two feet deep.

I would use this method when fishing tight to islands or on top of shallow bars, only to know if the water is deep enough to hold carp. If the float shows when cast in position then the water is obviously too shallow to hold carp under normal conditions. Carp will get in incredibly shallow water under certain circumstances such as spawning, but if the idea is to get one or more fish feeding confidently we would ideally need at least two feet of water.

This method of plumbing proved particularly effective for me a couple of seasons ago at a forty acre gravel pit in the Colne Valley known as Springwood. Due to inefficient excavation of the gravel many years ago, the lake bed contained a huge underwater network of bars and plateaux, some only covered with a few inches of water; many times when I was fishing there I saw people fishing in water only inches deep. My preparation became invaluable and without doubt worth the time I invested in plumbing certain swims. Another interesting thing I noticed while plumbing the part of the lake containing islands is that in some cases the angle of drop-off between one side of the island and the other was totally different. One side was almost sheer, dropping into four feet of water, the other tapering out to form a shallow bar adjoining the next island along. The water close to the island on this side was only six inches deep!

This gives you a good idea as to how important this type of plumbing can be, under the right circumstances.

(2) Tying a large float on the end of the line with a heavy lead sliding on the line above it.

This is the type of plumbing that I use for 95% of the time; it is extremely accurate for giving you depths at anything up to one hundred yards range.

Simply cast the lead and float out the required distance, pull in the slack until the float hits the lead, then pay the line out a foot at a time until the float pops to the surface.

I'll take you through a typical plumbing cast on a fairly well established gravel pit which has trees on one or more banks. You are casting from the east bank towards to west, though the difference in the quantity of leaves you will find against windward side of any steep bars will depend on the season (September–February being the worst). This is only an imaginary cast but it will show you what you are likely to feel, when gravel pit fishing waters such as Savay, Harefield or Springwood.

A cast of one hundred yards puts you somewhere towards the middle or beyond. The line should be sunk immediately on a tight line and the float pulled back to the lead until it stops. Let us assume you have landed on smooth bottom, but the lead is hard to pull towards you. This is either silt or, more likely, decaying leaf. Continue pulling the lead towards you; suddenly you feel a bump. This is gravel or the broken ground at the side of a bar. Let the float up a foot at a time, say it's eight feet at the first gravel. Now pull the float down to the lead and move the lead towards you again. The bumps continue and a check on the depth confirms a gradual decrease in depth until you have three feet six inches, when suddenly the line falls slack. What you have done is climbed a slow tapering bar which has a much shearer side to it on your side. The lead has simply fallen off the top. The ground is now smooth and easy to pull the lead in a clean smooth gulley, excellent in winter, possibly kept clean by fish activity. Check the depth—six feet six inches, perfect. Carry on pulling in the lead, and for quite a time there are no movements on the tip, then tap tap—gravel again, but this time the lead jams up solid on a steep-sided bar, with the sheer edge on the other side. If you are careful you may free the lead without pulling it off the bar, in which case you may find a tapering side, on your side this time.

It will be easy for you to tell if you are fishing this particular area because you will find difficulty clipping the lead up tight as it will continually roll towards you. The only difference between a bar and a plateau is the area of flat gravel on the top, plateaux tending to be much larger as a rule and not necessarily connected to a long bar.

So now you have found some areas, try the same cast five degrees to the right and left, and so on, pin-pointing markers such as trees on the horizon to give you the casting line. Write it down, it will be worth the trouble.

This type of pre-season planning is invaluable but far more will be learnt when you actually begin to fish the water.

Assuming you are happy with where you are going to fish, I suggest picking at least two waters, as the big one you may be after could well get caught on the first day of the season and unless there are other fish you want to catch from the water you will need a back-up venue for at least three or four weeks to give it time to be confident again. Of course some fish do get caught with much smaller time lapses between captures, but as a general rule, three or four weeks is needed. You will now be thinking about whether to pre-bait.

Pre-baiting can be costly and is not always beneficial, especially if everyone is doing it. On the other hand if you intend to fish in a group with several other anglers, a baiting campaign may not be so expensive and if it's a totally new bait for the water it could be well worth it. I'll give you an example of a lake I and some friends pre-baited several years ago. The bait was tiger nuts, never used on the water before, so totally strange to the fish.

We began pre-baiting, not in the close season, but in August. Everytime we packed up fishing and reeled in our boilies, we put in about four pounds of tigers between us in all the known safe areas and holding trees. We weren't using them on the hook because each time we looked, none had been eaten. We still kept putting them in and this went on for about five weeks; still none had gone, then in one week, the lot had gone! We put more in, and the fish were on them straight away—they were having it. The rest is history, but we went on to have a mega-season, so the campaign had worked. As you can see, pre-baiting can be advantageous. With boilies, however, I do not usually bother to pre-bait a water that has received a lot of boilies in the past. Most round balls will now be automatically accepted as food, so an introduction to boilies is unnecessary.

Bait

Any of you who have already come across my writing on bait will know that my outlook on the bait scene is far from technical. I've never been one for sitting down with a calculator and working out equations to form any bait I've ever made.

Time may change me of course; who knows what the next decade has in store for us? But up to now I've always tried to make my baits with three main objectives in mind. Firstly—cost; unless I'm absolutely convinced that a certain product which happens to cost a fortune will actually put loads more fish on the bank I don't intend to waste untold money on it. I'll probably try it, but unless it's pretty instant that will be the end of it. I may miss a few opportunities with this philosophy but at the end of the day I already know baits which are consistent catchers, and I've been known to catch more than my fair share on them, so I'll stick with what I know. Perhaps that sounds a bit 'head in the sand' and I don't want it to sound that way, but what I'm saying is that you see an advert in a magazine, 'New aminotrace formula X' (made up name)—the latest technology, all mod cons—you know the sort of thing I mean. Well, I look at the product and then at the angler marketing it, and I think to myself, 'How can that bloke say that about it, I know he's never caught anything on it?' If I see him in the *Angling Times* each week with a thirty or a forty or even a carp of any description, then I may sit up and listen, but don't tell me that ingredient is the business when you haven't even caught anything on it yourselves.

It's the same with foreign fish to advertise baits, it's just not the same. French, Dutch or bloody Outer Mongolian are just not English fish, and the reason they are different is because of the pressure on our waters compared to theirs. We invented the thing, now we've pressured the fish to behave entirely differently from fish on a virgin water in the Canary Islands. I know I'll have people saying 'Last time I was at Cassein there were two hundred Englishmen fishing there'. Yes it is starting to feel the pressure now, and bait, rigs, location etc. will become more and more important, but it's not had twenty or thirty years of pressure like some of our waters in this country. I'm not knocking foreign fishing, each man to his own and I can see a great many attractions to fish these lovely waters abroad, all I'm saying is, it's not quite the same.

I seem to have gone on a bit so I'll return to my objectives on bait. The next is that it rolls easily. I hate making bait more than anything in fishing and the last thing I need is something which is a pain to roll.

However, fish meals in a pure state are difficult to roll and only by adding 'other' ingredients to them do we seem to be able to keep a clean roll with these baits. The last thing, and probably the most important thing, is palatability to the fish; I've got to be sure they will eat it. This is easily achieved by watching the fish in safe areas or even in the close season to a certain extent, although they do tend to eat almost anything at this time of year.

So those are the basic things I look for in a bait. I'm not too fussy about what type of bait I use—particles are great if they will have them, so are mixers and the like but boilies are what I do 90% of any fishing with, so that's what I intend to concentrate on in this section—the ingredients available, and how to formulate them into baits which follow the three objectives I've just mentioned. I don't intend to go into shelf life boilies, freezer baits or packet base mixes. They all will catch carp and I even have my own range of packet base mixes marketed through Catchum products, but they're really self explanatory. You just buy them and use them. If you haven't got loads of spare time for bait making or you go fishing on the spur of the moment, they are the baits for you. It all depends what you want to do. I can't vouch for the ready made boilies, I don't use them to any great extent. My base mixes definitely work, I use them myself and I won't use anything that doesn't catch.

I'll look at ingredients in three groups, although any one from a group can be used with any one from another group. It's just easier this way. Fish meals, bird foods and milk proteins, but in no order of preference, although they do seem to be heading that way. I'll start off with the dry powder ingredients and then go briefly into bait soaks, essences, and oils etc. which can be used with these items.

White Fish Meal

This is one of the main constituents of most of the very successful fish meal base mixes marketed recently. It is about 60%–70% protein and has an oil content somewhere in the region of 5%–10% depending on the type of fish used in the meal. Cod, whiting, haddock, ling and sprat are the basis of this very smelly ingredient, which also has a high level of lysine, an amino acid commonly known to be attractive to carp. To be truthful, I haven't used fish meals as much as I should have done recently, because I seem to have got bogged down with bird foods, but that will change this forthcoming season as the field testing that has just been done with some of my fish meal mixes has been staggering. You will need a binder with these coarse ingredients. There are various ones available—semolina, vitamealo and gluten are all pretty good. Semolina, although some people will tell you otherwise, is just as good as any, and it's the cheapest.

Shrimpmeal (Red and White)

This is not my most favourite of fish meals because of its coarseness and its buoyancy. That said, it is still a very useful ingredient if used correctly and most fish meal bases mixes will contain it. Its protein content falls around the 50% mark and not only does it have a very high oil content but it also has a very distinctive smell. Whereas I would use the white fish meal in anything up to 4oz of a one pound mix I would only be looking at an ounce or so of the shrimp just so to give the mix a more rounded feel to it, combined with the musky fish smell of the shrimp. I have had equally good results with either the white or the red but the red seems to smell anything up to half as much again to the white. It's also an ingredient I have used with protein baits to give them added buoyancy, and I much prefer it to the widely used sodium caseinate for this type of application.

Tuna meal is relatively new on the bait scene, but it's already proved itself to be a winner on all the waters it has been used on, especially in the Colne Valley and the Darenth area. Tuna is widely acclaimed by body builders and the like as an excellent nutrient source and its convertability to the carp is second to none. Just to get technical for a minute about the fish oil found in this and other similar meals, they do contain small quantities of DHA omega three, fatty acids which have been stabilised and will certainly promote growth and replenish any damaged tissue in fish especially the tail and fin areas. I don't intend to go into oils yet as these will be covered when I get on to bait soaks, but the use of these oils with the fishmeals have produced some quite amazing catches.

Crab and crustacean meals are also very popular high oil content meals. The meal comprises ground shell and carcass, along with a small quantity of crab or lobster flesh. Again the protein content is in the region of 60%.

So what other fishmeals can we use in smaller quantities? Sandeel, mackerel, capelin, sardine and anchovy are all very good. I won't go into all the various protein contents etc. of these meals, as they are all fairly similar, in the 60–70% level. The only thing I will say about them is that it is in my opinion beneficial to use several types of fishmeals in the same base mix. Each meal has a different amino-acid base and by using a variety of meals in the same mix any amino-acid deficiency in one meal can be supplemented by another meal's make up. You should have no problem rolling these baits as long as you use suitable binders; gluten, semolina or any of the calf milk replacers used at about 2–3 oz to the mix will be sufficient to provide a smooth roll from the mix.

What I've covered here are true fish meal mix ingredients, but spices, bird seeds or milk proteins can be added, and I'll cover those two bait types individually in the next part of the bait section.

Firstly, though, some fish meal recipes.

Fish Meal Recipes

Recipe 1
    3 oz white fish meal
    1 oz capelin meal
    1 oz sand eel meal
    2 oz wheat gluten
    2 oz semolina
    1 oz 30 mesh casein
    5 ml seafood flavour (Catchum)
    2 ml intense sweetener
    5 ml multi-flavour enhancer

Recipe 2
    4 oz white fish meal
    2 oz mackerel meal
    2 oz tuna meal
    2 oz wheat gluten
    3 oz vitamealo
    5 ml lobster essence
    2 ml anchovy flavour
    2 ml MSG

Recipe 3
    2 oz crab meal
    2 oz capelin meal
    2 oz tuna meal
    3 oz semolina
    2 oz rennet casein
    30 ml bulk oil
    5 ml salmon oil

Recipe 4
    3 oz white fish meal
    2 oz tuna meal
    1 oz lactalbumin

1 oz 30 mesh casein
2 oz semolina
2 oz Robin Red
20 ml tandoori spice bait soak

Recipe 5
3 oz tuna meal
1 oz mixed spices
2 oz lactalbumin
1 oz salmon meal
1 oz liver powder
2 oz semolina
10 ml birianni spice dip (Catchum)
2 ml intense sweetener

Recipe 6
3 oz white fish meal
1 oz crab meal
2 oz nectablend
2 oz lactalbumin
1 oz 30 mesh casein
2 ml mega mino bait soak
10 drops essential oil cassia
2 ml intense sweetener

Birdfoods

These are the ingredients I have been experimenting with over the last few years and the results have been very conclusive. I wrote about birdfoods in my last book and really my thoughts haven't changed so I shall include a couple of paragraphs which I wrote at that time and just to bring bird foods right up to date I'll include a couple of my latest recipes.

Birdfoods, simple or complex? What are they, and why do they work? There seem to be several trains of thought as to why these ingredients are working so well at the moment. Our 'bait experts' will tell us it is because they are 'high energy' or 'high fat' diets which are beneficial to the carps overall needs. Perhaps now that he has a surplus of protein, other dietary requirements are now sought after. I am inclined to believe this may be true to a certain degree, but my own personal view as to why these baits seem to be out-fishing other baits is that they are different—simply that.

With so many people now offering the fish milk proteins the fish just fancy a change. I like chips, but I don't want them everyday; and the woman working in the cake shop couldn't possibly eat another cake. Proteins are excellent baits and I still use them in certain applications but fish meals and bird foods offer the fish a change. On the whole bait manufacture is much simpler and cheaper. My own preference is simply to mix equal quantities of Red Factor, CeDe or Nectablend with semolina, adding the normal flavours, sweeteners and attractors, but the time consuming chore of weighing out small quantities of perhaps a dozen ingredients is now removed. The mix should be made slightly sticky for rolling so as to ensure against crumbling, and the addition of one of the many pre-digested amino compounds such as aqua-mino or Boots the Chemist minamino will add to the effectiveness of the bait. This will of course up the price of the bait and I must admit that I personally haven't felt the need to add these liquids, although some of my friends place great faith in them.

So what are bird foods and where are they obtained? The list of bird foods is vast, and even I have only scratched on the surface in exploring their use. Some may be used straight from the packet as the grains are small enough to be made into a paste. Others which contain much larger items such as beans, peas or large seeds would require milling to a finer powder. I have actually tried some of these but being a naturally lazy person, eventually gave up and returned to good old Nectablend and Martin Locke's seed mix, both of which are ready to roll. I shall however list all the available bird foods that I have come across, even if I haven't actually used them myself, and say one thing: the ones I have used have all worked, but some in the list may not. Don't blame me if you decide to do some pioneering. First some mixes I have used over the years, then a list of all the available seed mixes, most of which can be obtained direct from Haiths in South Humberside.

Recipe 1
  8oz Semolina
  8oz CeDe
  4ml Catchum Megaspice
  20ml Spice Sense Appeal
  2ml Intense Sweetener
  1/2 teaspoon Multiflavour Enhancer
  5ml Spice Appetite Stimulator
  1/4 teaspoon Orange Dye

Recipe 2
  6oz Nectablend
  2oz Robin Red
  2oz 80 Mesh Casein
  6oz Whitworths Semolina

5ml Squid Pike Attractor
5ml Catchum Steak and Kidney
5ml Savoury Appetite Stimulator
20ml Savoury Sense Appeal
4ml Protaste

Recipe 3
16oz Locke's Seed mix
2 drops Essential Oil of Black Pepper
2 drops Essential Oil of Paprika
1/2 teaspoon Multiflavour Enhancer
4ml Intense Sweetener
20ml Spice Sense Appeal
1/2 teaspoon Yellow Dye

Recipe 4
4oz Sluis Mynah Bird Food
4oz Sluis Universal
2oz Prosecto Insectivorous
3oz Vitamealo
8oz Whitworths Semolina
5ml Pukka Salmon
2ml Intense Sweetener

Recipe 5
8oz Red Factor
8oz Whitworths Semolina
8ml Chocolate Malt
4ml Intense Sweetener
20ml Regular Sense Appeal
1/2 teaspoon Megaspice

Recipe 6
3oz Nectablend
3oz Robin Red
2oz Lactalbumin
2oz Semolina
20ml Tandoora Spice Bait Soak

So there you have a few recipes that I have personally done well on over the last few years. If you wish to use a pre-digested amino liquid, simply drop the Sense Appeal and use 50ml of minamino or aquamino, which may sound like a lot, but it is very safe, and very attractive. I have actually seen friends of mine injecting it into their anti-tangle tubing along with a tiny amount of flavour and also soaking cotton wool inside a block end swim feeder, such is their conviction of its attraction properties.

Now the list of bird foods; some will be analysed at the end of the list.

Egg Biscuit Food	Foreign Finch Tonic Food
Nectablend	Condition Seed
PTX Budgie Softfood	Budgie Tonic Seed
Budgie Protein Food	Love Bird Mixture
Softbill Food	Rayreen Mazagan Mix
Prosecto Insectivorous	Moroccoean Canary Mix
CeDe Priming and Rearing Food	Canadian Canary Mix
Sluis	Australian Canary Mix
Sluis Mynah	Dakota Red Millet
Sluis Universal	Special Haiths Budgie Mix
Red Factor Canary Food	No 3 Budgie Mix
Fine Oystershell Grit	DeLuxe Haiths Canary Mix
Robin Red	British Finch Mix
Ready Mix Carophyll	Aviary Mixture
Spanish Pepper Mix	Parrakeet Mixture
Java Dove Mix	Carophyll Red
Kraker Tonic Grains	Songster Food

NB Some of these mixes require milling.

So as I said earlier some of these I haven't used to any great extent. Some that I have are explained below:

CeDe

CeDe is Dutch and is basically an egg food containing yellow egg yolk, biscuit, hemp, and a variety of small seeds. It contains red and yellow Carophyll and is used for the priming and rearing of canaries.

Nectablend

Egg yolk, biscuit, honey and many different vitamins make the basics for Nectablend. It is described as a rearing food and has a protein content of 14%, a fat content of 5% and many vitamins and minerals. Depending on where you get it from, you will also find it contains a variety of small seeds such as Rape, Niger, Teazel, Linseed (high in oil content), Hemp, Lettuce, Blue Hawseed (Poppy seed) and Sesame—an excellent all rounder.

BAIT 23

Red Factor

Red Factor gets its name from the addition of water soluble Carophyll which is added to this priming and conditioning mix. Interestingly this mix also contains a small quantity of several essential oils. This one has been a 'killer' in the Colne Valley.

PTX

This is a 32% animal protein mix, with added honey and vegetable protein. The meat meal used for the base gives a high oil content along with a comprehensive spectrum of vitamins and minerals.

So there you have it, the bird foods which I and friends of mine have been using for the past few seasons. It is of course possible to make your own if you really wanted to, so here are a list of ingredients for the DIY anglers amongst you:

Ground Egg Biscuit	Niger Seed
Millet Seed	Oats
Canary Seed	Groats (de-husked oat)
Rape Seed	Chicory
Linseed	Fine Oyster Shell
Hempseed	Carophyll
Poppyseed	Cress Seed
Teazels	White Lettuce
Crushed Sunflower	Gold of Pleasure
Crushed Safflower	Pine Nuts (ground)
Paddy Rice	Pinhead Oatmeal
Buck Wheat	

High Nutrient Value Ingredients

Caseins

Edible acid or rennet seem to be the two types of casein I see most commonly in the retail trade but within those two names are a whole host of variants, such as mesh and country of origin which are all worth considering when contemplating the use of casein in the bait. Firstly, mesh: the lower the number the coarser the powder. 30 mesh is about the coarsest we will use, and 200 mesh is about the finest. I like either to use 30 or 80 mesh. 30 mesh gives a harder bait. Casein is the primary protein of milk with a protein content in the region of 90%. I used to use a type of casein called 'Scottish Pride' but the availability of the mesh I used has now decreased to such a degree that I have only seen very fine meshes in the last few years. These days I see casein imported from Holland, France and New Zealand. It's hard to say if one is better than another. As long as it's good quality and within its 'use by' date I can't see any problems using it. The casein which is readily available to the carp angler is manufactured by precipitation, the condensed deposition of solids from a solution. The two mediums used for our caseins are lactic acid (lactic casein), the acid formed in sour milk and rennet (rennet casein), the curdled milk found in the stomach of an unweaned calf.

It's not a bad ingredient as long as you are careful of your supplier, but I have heard of cases of bad casein and I know several anglers that have put unsuccessful seasons down to poor casein and now refuse to touch the stuff.

Calcium Caseinate

This is one of my favourite HNV ingredients, on an equal par with lactalbumin. I have had excellent catches just on a combination of these two mixed with either bird foods or fish meals. It is soluble lactic acid precipitated, then treated with an alkaline salt. Its protein content is extremely high, around 96% and I used to buy it straight from the chemist, before it became commercially available from tackle shops over ten years ago. Then it went under the trade name of Casilan.

It is excellent for the fining down of coarse mesh casein and when combined with this ingredient the biological value to carp (what the carp can actually get out of it) is increased greatly. It's heavy, it rolls well, and has fairly good binding qualities.

Sodium Caseinate

Not one of my favourites this one, although once again it is around the 96% protein level. Many people add this to the bait to increase the buoyancy, but it's so sticky I find it practically impossible to use unless you only use very small amounts, when I wonder if it is worth using at all. Rennet precipitated is very light: open the bag and half of it ends up your nose—the other half down your trousers. Some people swear by it; I just swear at it: enough said.

Lactalbumin

Excellent, a must for a balanced HNV bait, providing you with a more complete amino acid profile. Easily digestible, of New Zealand origin. I have witnessed a much greater involvement with this ingredient over the past couple of years, many people using more of this than casein in the mix. I've never had any problems with this one but I am informed that this ingredient in particular suffers from ageing, and the shelf life for this, as with most milk derivatives, is only about three months. Some bait companies are now date stamping their bags, which is a good thing, and about time too, if you ask me. Fred Wilton liked it; it's around 85% protein, the secondary protein from milk and excellent when combined with fish meals.

Soya Powders

Soya isolate (85% protein), soya flour (50% protein) and full fat soya (38% protein) are the three principal types on the market. They are fairly self explanatory soya bean by-products, high in oil content and excellent flavour carriers.

Pruteen

I don't know whether this product is still available but it did become very popular over the past few years as an alternative to the milk proteins. This product, manufactured by ICI as a food supplement for cattle is a whole diet and contains a high protein percentage, around 75%. It is a bacterial growth of a single celled nature which when centrifugated is separated, then dried and granulated. It has a high biological value when used separately or combined with any of the three main base mix types.

Egg Albumin

The dried white of the egg—85% protein with good coagulating properties and when used in large enough amounts can reduce the boiling time on your bait. This would be beneficial in that flavours and additives are not boiled away so much and that vitamins etc., which are de-natured by heat, are less affected.

That just about covers the HNV's so here are a few recipes for you to try, starting with the most expensive and ending with the ones that I use, the cheapest.

Recipe 1
6 oz mesh edible casein
2 oz Lactalbumin
2 oz Egg albumin
2 oz Calcium caseinate
1 oz Liver powder
1 oz Soya isolate
5 ml Sweet bait enhancer

20 ml Dairy bait soak
5 ml Cream flavour
2 ml Intense sweetener

Recipe 2 (2 mixes)
4 oz 80 mesh edible casein
4 oz 30 mesh edible casein
4 oz Lactalbumin
2 oz Powdered seaweed kelp
2 oz Powdered fish oil
3 oz Calcium caseinate
3 oz Soya isolate
2 oz Vitrex mineral supplement
20 ml Tandoori bait soak
5 ml mega spice

Recipe 3
3 oz 30 mesh edible casein
2 oz Lactalbumin
2 oz Liver powder
2 oz Semolina
2 oz Calcium caseinate
20 ml Spice/Liver bait soak
10 ml Davina
5 ml Steak and kidney flavour
2 ml Intense sweetener

Recipe 4
3 oz 30 mesh edible casein
3 oz Lactalbumin
2 oz White fish meal
1 oz Robin Red
3 oz Semolina
2 oz Liver powder
20 ml Biriani bait dip
10 drops essential oil ylang ylang
2 ml Intense sweetener
10 ml Sweet bait enhancer

Recipe 5
2 oz 30 mesh edible casein
2 oz Lactalbumin
2 oz Calcium caseinate
6 oz Semolina

5 ml Multi flavour enhancer
20 ml Powdered seaweed kelp
20 ml Liquid liver
10 ml Megamino bait soak
2 ml Salmon oil

Recipe 6 (2 mixes)
  2 oz 30 mesh edible casein
  2 oz 80 mesh edible casein
  2 oz Lactalbumin
  2 oz Calcium caseinate
  10 oz Semolina
  4 oz Nectablend
  2 oz Tuna meal
  50 ml Minamino
  10 ml Tandoori bait soak
  10 drops essential oil cassia
  5 ml Multi flavour enhancer

Odds 'n' Sods

LIVER POWDER—Rich in amino acids and nucleotide enhancers, an excellent additive; use up to 3 oz in the mix.

WHEAT GLUTEN—90% protein, excellent binding properties, used a lot with fish meals. Add 2 oz to the mix.

LACTOPRO—Creamy, high sugar content, good skinning properties, similar to vitamealo, nuckamel, dairy lac and calpro. Up to 4 oz in the mix.

MOLASSES MEAL—Ground sugar beet or cane, 30% sugar content, very underestimated.

NUT MEALS—Peanut, tiger nut, hazel nut or cashew nut, finely ground, high protein and oil content. You may experience some problems rolling this one, but try 3 oz of gluten.

FEATHER MEAL—Excellent, especially the grey meal, distinctive aroma, musty fragrance, 90% protein—up to 4 oz in the mix.

WHEAT GERM—Rusk from the outside of wheat, 35% protein, high in roughage, you will certainly see them 'bubblin'' in the morning if you use much of this in the bait.

TROUT PELLET—Whole diet used for rearing trout. 40–50% protein. Not one of my favourites.

VITAMIN AND MINERAL SUPPLEMENTS—Equivite pellets, Equivite supplement and codlivine were the most widely used, but many companies are now formulating their own vitamin and mineral supplements. If you sit in Wilton's corner I suppose you must include some in the bait; results are inconclusive. Incidentally Biotin, the crystalline vitamin that you can find in yeast, controls growth, and yeast is a well known attractor even if it seems to have lost its popularity.

POWDERS—Powdered egg, liver products and cheese powder; liver has been a 'killer' on many lakes and I believe it is still very underestimated. Cheese powder in its various forms is now becoming more widely used; remember casein is the basis of cheese. I have used several different cheese powders in the past. All were very effective, highly stimulative and have an interesting taste and smell. The best stuff is actual powdered cheese, not the synthetic imitation. I use up to 2 oz in the mix, but a teaspoon can be detected.

SEMOLINA—My favourite ingredient; easy to roll, very cheap and can be used with or without eggs. It is high in carbohydrates, which are essential for energy. It is the hard grains left after milling wheat flour. As long as your attractors are effective this bait will keep going and going and I haven't ever found that people using boilies which cost two pounds each have out-fished my semo baits. It can be used as seventy five per cent of the bait, or as little as an ounce. It can be mixed with any of the other ingredients already mentioned. It's very heavy and aids putting your free samples out. It binds well and will not alter the flavour of the bait as some ingredients will. I would still recommend the addition of casein, as the baits are not quite hard enough without it. All pasta can be used in the ground form.

RICE—Rice is widely used and can be purchased already ground. Rice is the seed of an oriental marsh grass which is an annual cereal crop grown in hot climates. It is high in starch and carbohydrates. I recommend 2 oz in the mix; another cheap flavour carrier which provided a useful addition to Semolina based baits.

Well, that's basically the ingredients which are commonly used on the waters I fish. I have tried to explain them in anglers' language, not in the chemical jargon.

Sweeteners

MALTOSE—This is sugar produced by hydrolysis of starch under the action of malt; this disaccharide is half as sweet as sucrose, the normal household sugar.

A Savay mirror of 31-08 taken in October 1986.

The business end of a 34-12 Springwood fish.

A Springwood 34.

A superb Savay upper 20.

Two fat sods!

Not a monster but worth catching in the snow.

35-08 – the Fox Pool 'Parrot'.

A 31-12 taken at close range in winter 1985.

Almost 30, only an ounce to spare!

FRUCTOSE—Sugar from fruit; sold under the name 'Dietade', this sugar is one of my favourites; very sweet.

LACTOSE—The sugar found in milk; excellent when used in milk protein or semolina baits. The combination of dextrose and galactose forms this sweetener.

DEXTROSE—The dextro-rotary form of glucose obtained by acid hydrolysis of starch. Available in crystal or fine powder; almost as sweet as sucrose.

GLYCERINE—Colourless, sweet, viscous liquid formed as a by-product in the saponification of fats. A flavour base with excellent enhancing properties; use about 5 ml in the mix.

MOLASSES—A very underestimated sweetener; pure molasses is the uncrystallised syrup drained from raw sugar. The syrup is obtained from the sugar in the process of refining treacle.

SUCROSE—Common household sugar obtained from sugar cane and sugar beet.

Enhancers

Flavour enhancers are one of the small groups which really are being developed for the carp angling world. Taking the nucleotide and glutamate enhancers as a base, concentrated extracts, cheese powders and spices such as garlic are being mixed to provide the carp anglers with a different enhancer blend for all types of bait. Nucleotide enhancers are very popular and are said to cover a much wider band of enhancement compared with monosodium glutamate. I still prefer MSG and use it with sweet or savoury baits. The reason for this is that nucleotide enhancers are up to one hundred times as strong as MSG and I feel this concentration is too strong. I use half a teaspoonful of MSG to a ten ounce mix. It's simply added to the eggs and distributed evenly when the eggs are whisked. If you use pure nucleotides, particularly disodium inosinate and disodium guanylate which are suited to our requirements, you will only require a very small amount, about a fiftieth of a teaspoon, which is not easy to measure or distribute. Some bait suppliers now supply the nucleotides in a carrier which is easier to measure, but I'm still never one hundred per cent sure what quantity of the pure ingredient I am adding. Nucleotides are compounds of the phosphate group linked to sugar. Nucleosides are the compounds of sugar with a heterocyclic base, MSG is the neutral salt of L-glutomic acid. Most of the crisps and savouries you eat will contain this ingredient for flavour enhancing. If it's good enough for us to eat, it's good enough for carp. Incidentally, I don't see so many foodstuffs containing descriptions of nucleotide enhancers on the packet.

POWDERED FISH OIL—Bleached white powder, high fat trout diet, excellent ingredient—up to 2 oz in the mix.

POTATO PROTEIN—Don't know anyone who has ever used it.

KELP—Read *Tiger Bay* if you want to know how I got on with this excellent additive.

WORM EXTRACT—Liquid free amino source, up to 10 ml to the mix.

MINAMINO/AQUAMINO—Liquid liver and spleen, high in amino acids, which is what they give to pregnant women to boost their diets. An excellent ingredient—use up to 50 ml in the mix.

POLLEN—Bee's pollen, it's supposed to be secret but we've been using it for years. It's expensive but an excellent attractor.

ROYAL JELLY—Another expensive one, high in nutrients. If you can afford to use it, give it a go. If not, join the club.

Particles

I'm going to include a bit about particles for three reasons: firstly I haven't seen an up-to-date look at particle fishing for many years, secondly they are a brilliant method of catching big carp which seems to be very neglected in the area I'm fishing and thirdly, with the introduction of the new oil and amino acid bait soaks currently in fashion, many of the particles we now regard as 'past it' or 'old hat' can easily be given a new lease of life.

I feel confident that a devastating new particle is just around the corner for those of you who wish to look hard enough, and when it comes, as I'm sure it will, some fantastic results will be achieved on it, just as it did with the great particles of the last twenty years. How many of you remember first using corn for carp some fifteen odd years ago— mind blowing! They couldn't get enough of it. What about peanuts and maples, brilliant sport, then came the tiger nut and I doubt there will be many people around who haven't used tigers. They were without doubt a 'killer' bait. Such were their devastating effect on carp fishing that they were banned on some waters, much the same as hemp used to be banned on some waters as they used to think the fish became addicted to it. Roach never were addicted to it, they just loved it, and so do carp. So what have we got to look forward to? I wish I had a crystal ball, but I haven't and I just don't seem to have the time these days to experiment.

Most of the field work I do now is restricted to the close season; come the season I've got to know that I've got it right. I can't afford to be sitting on these big fish waters without the firm knowledge that my bait will catch, so the close season is spent researching new flavours and testing new mixes. Particles are a vast range of items many of which are still to be tried. What about pickled onions? Don't laugh, you could fish a big popped-up epicure over the top of a bed of silver skins. Would it catch, I wonder?—might even give it a try. Beetroot, diced swede, olives—the list is endless. Someone out there somewhere has probably given them a try already, but what about ten people all baiting with a new particle? Who's to know what lies around the corner? Could there be another sweetcorn or tiger nut. I think there almost certainly is, and more than one, and I'll make a prediction: in the next decade a new particle will come out that is the best yet!

Back to reality and the present day, let's have a look at some of the particles we know catch fish, and how we can give them a new lease of life with bait soaks, oils and flavourings.

Tiger Nuts

Wow! Do the fish like these or what? They are singularly the most exceptional bait I have ever used. For me they were even better than corn, maybe because I was in at the start with the nuts but missed the first exciting years with corn. They are simple to prepare, improved with a bit of age and the fish love them. My method of preparation is to soak the nuts in a solution of water, bulk oil, e.g. soya bean oil or white fish oil combined with a little liquid liver. Alternatively use one of the bait soaks. Leave them for about a day then boil them in the solution for about half an hour to an hour. Then tip the whole lot, liquid and nuts into a big bait bucket and they are ready to use. If you are fishing in the margins or snags you can actually tip some of the solution in with the loose feed; it will quickly dissipate and provide an attractive cloud for fish to home in on. You can flavour them if you wish and I have always found sweet sickly flavours the best with tigers, such as maple, scopex, butter or cream. I've included a couple of rig drawings which would still be the type of rig I would use for all my particle fishing, perhaps with a slight modification in the shape of a bent hook.

Other Nuts

Peanuts, hazel nuts and brazils: peanuts have, of course, been widely used in the past, and most people will be familiar with their use, but nuts such as hazels and brazils are now becoming much more popular, the only problem being their price which is quite extortionate. However, fishing a brazil over the top of peanut can produce increased action, and this is a method I have seen being used quite frequently. Hazels tend to be quite buoyant and although I haven't used them myself, I believe this buoyancy can be overcome by soaking.

Maize

Once extremely effective here in this country wherever it was used, this particle has now become very popular with anglers fishing abroad during the close season in places such as Holland and France. Carp tend to get very pre-occupied with maize once it takes off. As with many of these particles the best results are often achieved with germination: something to do with the production of Maltose from the starch found in maize, this sweet vegetable sugar is very attractive to carp, so it's best to soak the maize until it begins to sprout, then cook it in the pressure cooker. The bait soaks and flavours are then added and allowed to soak into the kernels. A small piece of poly fished along side a couple of grains will produce good presentation.

Beans

I'm going to lump all the beans together for the purpose of this piece due to lack of space. Kidneys, black-eyes, soya beans, limas and bolotti beans, will all catch fish with the right application. They all work better flavoured as they are pretty bland on their own, and savoury or spice flavours seem to be the most effective. Just a simple boil up in an old saucepan is sufficient to make beans usable, and you can even boil the beans in soup to add a nice mellow flavour to them.

Seeds

Hemp and daris are the two main mass baited seeds I have used in the past and both are excellent catchers. I usually soak the seed overnight in a liquid liver solution, then boil for about half an hour. Once the fish get on these small baits little can put them off. Chopped boilies mixed with the hemp and boilies fished over the top can be a devastating method.

Ready Mades

I can't really ignore these baits totally because on some waters, where they have been used extensively the fish that these baits have taken has been amazing. Bernard Loftus on Harefield immediately comes to mind, his results were quite staggering, and all caught on Richworths—Tutti-Fruttis, I believe. Many of the country's premier waters went the same way as well; Darenth is another example. So why is it that a bait which is so nutritionally inferior to the top of the range HNV's out fishes them hands down? There are a couple of trains of thought on this one. Availability seems to be the main one. If everyone is throwing in Richworths or Maestros or whatever the fish get used to finding them all over the lake and get on them purely because they are a readily available food source. That's what our HNV bait experts tell us. On the other hand they also tell us that a good bait will always out fish a crap bait in the end. This may be true, but how many fish do we let Noddy in the next swim catch before either we 'get on the Richworth's' or out fish him on our supa-doopa HNV? Chances are he will have emptied the lake and moved on before the HNV 'out fishes' him!

So what do we conclude? Well, what I seem to conclude is that the fish are not as clever as we make them out to be. If they can recognise the best, availability shouldn't have anything to do with it. Why is it that on some waters, and I've heard some well known anglers say this, 'You can't get a bite on anything else'. If HNV's etc. are so good why is that so?

I can't really give you a satisfactory answer that will please both sides of the argument. I just think they like what they like; tigers, ready mades, mixers, they just like them and they do seem to go on liking them. The availability answer only holds water once you have got a lot of people putting them in. But what about the pioneer? In the example I quoted it was Bernard who went where man feared to tread and used them from the off. Granted once he had caught loads of fish on them others followed on and so made them available. But to begin with it was only him, and a few bags a session. No more bait than others were putting in around him but he was the one catching consistently. Now you've got Ritchie McDonald on the Streamselects. I fished with him a couple of times last season. He caught two, I caught nothing and he was on 'ready mades'. I fished with Kevin Maddocks, too. He caught fish of 25 lb, 35 lb and over 40 lb between January and the end of the season, every bait straight from the bag and all his own KM Maestro ready-made baits. Packed in oil and opened on the bank. I was there and I never had a bite. It makes you wonder, doesn't it? Catchum ready-mades caught an incredible amount of fish last year. I used them at Chigborough, as did most of the other people there, they loved them. So, regardless of what the experts tell us, let's not loose sight of the facts. Ready mades catch, of that there is no doubt. At the end of the day it all depends on whether you want to make them yourselves, or what you feel more confident with. I like to make my own, but not because I get more satisfaction out of what I catch, as some people say; that's rubbish. It's like saying I'll make my own tiger nuts or Mixers—it would take you forever and for what point? I would rather just open a bag and fish with them. I get just as much pleasure out of a thirty on nuts as I do on home-made boilies. The only reason I make my own is individuality; I make my own boilies as different from everyone else's as I can. If everyone is on red I use yellow; if everyone is on small boilies, I'll use big or vice-versa, just to be different because that is where my confidence lies.

Bait Soaks

These fall into several categories, from simple fish feed inducing oils, oil emulsions and flavour enhancers to the more complicated liquid amino acid compounds combined with appetite stimulating oils and resins. They are extremely popular at the moment and I would imagine that over the next two years almost every carp angler will be using them to a certain degree, I say to a certain degree because there are extremes with the use of this type of additive. You could use as little as 5 ml to a mix or with some of the soaks as much as 50 ml to a mix.

Liquid liver-based aminos, for instance, like the popular mina mino, can be eaten in its pure state; pregnant mums are given it to boost their diets, as I've already said, so it won't be harmful to the fish. Some of the oils also can be used in quite large amounts but it is far safer to leave the correct dosage to those who know and not to think that the more in the mix the better, which is not the case. If the research for a bait soak has been done correctly someone with a sound chemical level background will have formulated the mix and set the safety levels. I suggest these correct levels are followed. I have recently been involved with certain formulations and the words our chemist is coming up with just leave me with my mouth open, so the actual levels are set by someone in the know and that's what I stick to regardless of whether I think it is enough or not. So what are the soaks? Well, as I said you can use a simple fish oil and just add it to the mix and soak your hook baits in it, or you can go for one of the complex mixtures which are available—I think Richworth have some in their new list. Maestro boilies also have a new range and of course I have the Obsession range marketed through Catchum Products, so there are quite a few to choose from, and quite a variety of types such as spice, dairy, fish, meat and fruit, so all the various types of flavours are covered.

Individual labelling of the bait soak can easily be achieved by adding 5 ml of your own individual flavour to every 100 ml of the bait soak, so unique soaks and dips are quite simple to form.

I have been having excellent results just lately with a combination of Spice Birdseed and essential oil marine mix combined with a spice and fish bait soak. If you haven't tried them yet they are certainly worth a try. Kevin Maddocks took three tremendous fish this winter as I've already said on packet boilies soaked in the Maestro Booster Dips, and if he can catch them . . .! Only kidding, Kevin!

Rob with 'Arfur' (tail) at 27 pounds.

Don't forget — discarded line kills birds and other wild animals

Location

I am going to split location into two halves, summer and winter but many of the rules which apply to one can just as easily apply to the other. The one 'rule' in carp fishing that you can be certain of is that there are no rules, just guidelines. Carp can do the weirdest things on certain days, quite out of character to what you would expect, like for instance being caught in really shallow water on the coldest days, not at all where you would expect them to be, but it happens, and everyone has to think again. So the observations I have made are not rules but only guidelines.

I'm going to start with winter because I feel that not only is it the most difficult time to locate carp, but also the most important. During the warmer months carp will be continually on the move, cruising and basking in the heat of the day, visiting safe areas and snags and moving into bays and quiet corners in the evenings. The margins are also frequented to a great extent, something which seems to be neglected in these days of horizon rods and 'Exocet' leads. Also feeding will not necessarily be concentrated to one particular time of the day. It could happen anytime, and with a change of approach say from bottom fishing to surface fishing an additional fish may be taken. So what I'm saying is that in the summer fish could visit your swim at any time of the day and you always have a chance. Winter is different, the carp will not be anywhere near so active even on the warmest of days. They won't be on the move anywhere as much as in summer so if you're not somewhere pretty close to where they are laying up, you probably won't get fish moving in and out of your baited areas.

There are definitely winter hotspots on all the lakes I have fished in the past—areas which seem to produce the majority of winter action regardless of the pressure they receive. These spots may be close to snags or close to distant islands, deep silty gullies, in between bars and on one lake, Springwood, actually on a couple of relatively shallow gravel bars at about forty/fifty yards range. Old decaying weed beds or dying beds of lily pads are another favourite winter area, and if you are to catch consistently through the colder months it is essential for you to discover these areas. Past knowledge of productive winter swims is invaluable if you can gather it. Watching others fishing the lake you are on will give you a good idea.

You can learn just as much from a good angler in the wrong swim as you can from him in the right one, so be observant of any action that occurs while you are on the water. This is far more easily achieved if you fish with a group of other anglers, like myself who fishes with the same four anglers all year, regardless of the venue. Someone is bound to see something—a back breaking the surface or a few bubbles which appear to be on the move. These are the subtle things which can lead you to success in winter location.

Summer should prove much simpler in the case of location. In hot weather many fish will be on or near the surface and a quick look round from any convenient spotting trees is certainly worth the trouble. I always try to be vigilant at dawn and dusk as these seem to be the two main times when fish will be on the move. Typical signs are fish crashing or lunking out of the water although many times a fish will be able to lift two thirds of its body clear of the water only to slide silently back leaving hardly a trace. Look out for 'flat spots' on windy days, which could be fish moving through or close to the surface layers which cause these breaks in the ripple, also just after or during a storm especially if the water is really being pounded by the rain. I have always found carp very active in this situation probably due to the influx of oxygen into the upper layers. Fish may also be located as they move around island margins and also the tops of shallow bars so this is always worth spending some time on if the lake contains these features.

Unlike winter when wind, in my opinion has little or no effect on the movement of carp, warm summer winds certainly will move some fish, most noticeably on the big open gravel pits, though the fish may not necessarily move in the direction of the wind. This has proved the case at Savay Lake, when I was fishing it. Due to the pressure put on fish when a new wind came up, the fish began to wise up to this and in many instances moved to the back of the wind. As a general rule though I would be far more confident fishing into the wind than behind it. Quite why the fish move with a new wind is something that we as anglers can only guess at. Tiny food particles or higher oxygen levels against and around the end being hit by the wind is a theory which has been around since the year dot. I'm not so sure it's either of those, but move they do, so it always pays to be mobile on the big pits.

Just to talk of Savay for a moment, several years ago the wind was such a deciding factor that the weather centre was phoned regularly and at the first sign of a new wind the syndicate would try to be one step ahead of the fish and they would move quickly and bait a swim in anticipation of fish moving to the area. This method was exploited to great effect by some of the top catchers of the time, but as I said this method is not so effective at Savay these days, though it is still worth doing if you are all fishing the water.

That should have given you a basic insight into the location of fish, but the one and only method to true success is to spend time on the water; watercraft can only be learnt, not bought from the tackle shop, like almost everything else you will need.

When you arrive at the water, have a look around. This may not always be possible on today's 'high pressure' waters; it's first come, first served, and for most of us it's really a matter of taking the best of what swims are left. However let's assume you have picked your swim, for whatever reason. Perhaps you have seen fish or perhaps you haven't but are confident you have picked the right spot. The first thing to do if you haven't seen fish is to find out something about what lies below the water line. The section on plumbing should help you there. If you have seen fish or are still seeing fish I wouldn't go slinging a float about out there. At least spend a little while with a bait as near to the fish you are seeing as possible. I wouldn't put any free offering out either as this can prove sudden death in some cases, so just try a lone bait or a stringer roughly in the area of the fish. How long you fish like this is really a matter of choice—or rather it's a matter of patience. If there are fish out there feeding then this method combined with the right bait and rig should be as good as any, but it is all too easy to think 'I'll just ping a few baits out so they get their heads down'. It might work, but if it doesn't chances are your fish will be on their toes (or fins) and move out of the area. Patience is the best answer, but I know it's not easy. I usually give it a couple of hours then pile the bait in, but I can't remember many instances where this has worked, and I always end up wishing I had given it another couple of hours.

If you haven't seen fish but are convinced you are in the right spot, have a feel around, see what features you have got to fish on, then if you are still sure it's the right spot set up for the session. You may already know what the swim has to offer; all the better, no disturbance has got to be a bonus. Although I'm not convinced it makes that much difference, chances are if you do spook anything out of the swim curiosity will bring it back eventually. I suppose it all rests on how long you are going to be there. Ground-baiting will be the next thing you will be thinking of and this is another big one, if not the whole key to successful session. No one gets it right all the time, but the anglers that get it right consistently are the ones that seem to do the best. How much to put in is really the question, and this is a question that there is no simple answer to.

I'm really going to have to break this question down into several different areas, as a difference in bait type, fish head count and season can all make a difference. I'll start with head count, in other words the number of fish likely to visit your swim at any one time during the session and I'll also start with summer/autumn.

As a general rule during the warmer months I will put in about one pound of boilies or two pounds of particles at the start of a session. The difference between the two is quite a lot and this is due to the carp being able to pass beans, peas and nuts straight through themselves while feeding. Boilies, especially protein and HNV's will fill the fish up very quickly. Now as we are talking about fishing for big carp the chances are that we will only have a maximum of two or three fish in the swim at any one time. If, however, you were fishing a water with an extremely large head of big carp you would need a lot more bait to hold the shoal and I have used up to five pounds of boilies at the start of the session, which was when I had upwards of twenty/thirty pound fish moving into the swim during a short evening feeding spell. In this particular instance I just couldn't put in too much bait and everything was cleared up in a frenzied half hour just on dark, my first four nights on the water resulting in a fish a night—three thirties and a twenty nine, but this is quite heavy baiting and as a rule I would be using less. We used to use a rule of fifty boilies to a fish, but boilie size seems to vary so much these days, some people using baits the size of peas and others the size of a chicken's egg so that rule seems a bit pointless. So give them a pound and if you have any action I would top up with another eight ounces after each bite.

Winter is a much harder time to judge the quantity of your ground-bait, it is also one of the most important times to get it right. During the summer, overbaiting can often be counterbalanced by other types of fish on the bait or even one or two greedy fish. In winter, however, I have found it sudden death to over-bait, but on the other hand I have still used quite a lot of bait in winter when I knew it was right to do so. These days I feel happier with a small stringer or even a lone bait rather than over baiting the area.

So that's a very rough guide to ground-baiting; at the end of the day it's all relative to the individual water you are fishing, and getting it right can only be achieved by trial and error.

So let's quickly recap the things we have gone over. Choosing the water, pre-baiting and close season preparation; location, plumbing, and ground baiting. That just about covers the basics to start fishing, now let's talk about two of the key ingredients which when combined with location can bring you success:— bait and rigs. Then I'll go on to give you examples of a couple of memorable sessions when all these things were put together and brought the right results in both summer and winter.

Question Time with Sir Robin

As most of you well know I do quite a number of meetings and conferences up and down the country throughout the winter and close season. It is usual at these events for me to do a slide show for about an hour or so and then to have a question and answer session. A familiar pattern has emerged during the year and the questions seem to take on the theme of any of the latest developments that are in use on the waters I fish. The questions are always up-to-date, and I no longer get asked the questions which were so important five years ago, like for instance how to make microwaved pop-ups, or how much flavour do I use in a mix. Most people now know this, but it's the latest developments they wish to know about. It has occurred to me this nucleus of questions that I seem to get asked most about are well worth recording and answering in a short section in this book. These could well be the questions that are burning on the lips of carp anglers up and down the country and hopefully this book is being developed to answer many of your questions, so here are some of the questions I get asked all the time:

Question—The bent hook rig has received a lot of publicity since your book 'Fox Pool', but the carp in our water are nowhere near so careful as those in the waters you fish. Do you think we really need it, as we can still catch them on the other rigs?

Answer—I wish I had a pound for every question I've had to answer about the bent hook just recently, and this particular question came up twice in a fortnight from two very different places, firstly in Hull and then in Boxmeer at a Dutch conference held by Henk Bruin. The simple answer is that you probably don't need it, just the same as you didn't really need the hair rig when that first came out or protein bait or carbon rods; the list is endless. You don't really need them but on the other hand you have got nothing to lose by keeping abreast of the times, and if at the end of the day it's only put one more fish a season on the bank for you it was still worth it. I remember my resistance to the hair when I first saw it used; I was catching well on side hooked baits, why change?

It wasn't long before you could hardly catch anything without the hair in one form or another, so that's why you should use it. It will simply put more fish on the bank for you.

Question—What hook link material do you use and why?

Answer—Over the past few years I seem to change my hook link material about every two seasons as something new, which I think is good, comes on the market. This question is really a bit like the last one. Why should I use Gamabraid when I can catch them on Dacron? Well, in my opinion hook link materials are getting better and better as each new braided composite comes on the market. I never liked the original multistrand, I used to get too many tangles, but these later braids like Gamabraid, Silkworm and Merlin do seem to have excellent properties in both abrasion resistance and suppleness. They also seem to have overcome the wet knot strength problems they had originally and they also seem to be getting finer in diameter. So that's what I suppose I shall be using in the next couple of seasons, although for the past two years I have been using Berkeley braided nylon and have found this material, although a bit thick, to be an excellent hook link material.

Question—You said you use heavy leads in the four or five ounce size and you mentioned the use of round leads; why is this?

Answer—The answer to this one will already be covered in the book but I'd still like to cover this area again as I feel that the effectiveness of even the best rig in the world still rests on the lead to hook the fish. I'm talking about fixed lead rigs now, which is what I use for almost all of my fishing. The only time I use a running lead is when I am fishing up against snags and I wish to know the moment the bait is picked up. In this case a running lead with a light bobbin will give immediate indication and I can pull into the fish and try to prevent it getting amongst the snags. If you had a fixed lead on in these circumstances the fish would prick itself on the lead and bolt straight into the snags before you have any chance of preventing it.

So I use fixed leads for most of my sessions and I use big leads, five ounces for anything up to 100 yds and four ounces for anything over 100yd. The rods I use, the Leslie's 13ft, 2lb 9oz, will cast fives easily up to 100yd but you really need to wind the rod up when going over that distance so a four ounce is a bit kinder to the rod and more efficient.

The reason for the big leads is obvious; as the fish picks up the hook it pulls against the lead. The stronger that resistance, the better hooking you will get.

So why round leads? Well it was my good friend Steve Allcott that really got the ball rolling (excuse the pun) with this type of lead. It's common sense really, if you have a long lead or a torpedo shaped lead it is possible for the fish to lift one end of the lead a small distance before the total weight of the lead takes effect. That small pivoting of the lead can give the fish just that chance it needs to reject the hook. With a round lead, as soon as the hook hits the lead it hits all the weight straight off and total hooking is instant. Watch out for the round leads, though I suppose by the time this book gets out quite a few leads will be on the market.

Question—What are bait soaks, what type of bait are they best used with and how can I make my own?

Answer—Bait soaks are a solution made up of various liquids, which can be added straight to the mix, in with the eggs, and can be used neat with the hook baits. The hook baits are simply soaked in a small container which holds the liquid, while you are fishing or before you go fishing. There are various types around ranging from simple fish oil soaks to the more complex Catchum soaks which incorporate bulk oils such as fish, vegetables, and nut oils combined with liquid amino acid compounds based around liquid liver and spleen, essences and/or essential oils in very small ratios, such that the soak is acceptable to the fish in its raw state. There are currently soaks on the market for fish type flavours, spice and essential oil flavours, dairy and sweet confectionery flavours. To these soaks you add your own individuality with a flavour of your own choice.

They can be used with almost any type of bait, particles, Chum Mixers or boilies and with almost any type of boilie, fish meal, bird food or protein. They are certainly something which has taken off just recently and some quite incredible catches have been made with them. There is some concern about the weight that the fish are putting on, on the waters that have received substantial amounts of the oil soaks, and people are wondering abut the long term effects of this almost unnatural growth rate. Of course, it's impossible to predict this long term effect, but it's certainly not the first time we have witnessed this surge in weight gain. It happened when protein HNV's hit the scene, and the carp shot up in weight then. I remember these very same questions being asked but we are now in a position to say 'Well, it didn't seem to do them any harm', and some of the ingredients helped the fish mend damaged tissue and repair torn fins etc.

These bait soaks are known to contain certain things which will also repair tissue and fins as I've already said, so let's hope they enjoy this new diet with its obvious advantages and we can go on to catch bigger fish in the process. I wonder now if the weight gain, supposing it is artificial, will be lost just as easily when these new baits eventually lose their devastating effect? As to making your own, this is very simple and by trial and error with the liquids I mentioned earlier you should be able to come up with soaks and dips just as good as the ones already marketed. However, I would imagine the initial outlay would be very expensive, just to get all the liquids to make your soaks, and if it's only normal quantities of the emulsion that you require, buying a ready made solution would seem more practical.

Question—Why do you catch so many big carp?

Answer—This is a serious question that I have been asked many many times, and the answer is simple. I fish waters with big carp in them. That's it, it's that simple. If the fish aren't in your lake you are not going to catch them. I don't catch many carp during the season, but I usually have my share of big ones, because I am willing to wait for quite considerable times for the fish I am after to come along. In fact I catch more fish in the close season than I do the season. I fish places like Farlows at Iver in Buckinghamshire and Broadlands in Hampshire which contain good heads of doubles and a sprinkling of bigger fish. It's now that I try out new baits and rigs and gain the confidence I need in these things to see me through the season. If I try out a bait and it catches ten times as much as anyone else is using I am confident it will work on some of the big fish waters, given time. A carp is a carp on any water; the only thing that makes most big fish waters hard is that there are few carp in the water. Last season I fished three waters where the total known head count is thirty three fish, in all three waters added together. Now obviously you aren't going to have a string of fish to your credit at the end of the season but if you catch a couple you have done well. It's not everyone's cup of tea though and I know some of my friends who are in excellent big fish waters but don't fish them because they just must catch something every time they go out.

   That's why I fish easier waters in the close season; it gets it out of my system, I get a bend in the rod, loads of action and come the season I'm ready to wait for a big boy. Big fish are no harder to catch than little ones, it's all down to the water.

Question—You seem to have changed your thoughts on bait just recently. In the past you have been an advocator of 'crap baits'. Why do we now see you with a range of baits some of which are not cheap?

Answer—I haven't changed my thoughts on baits at all really. I was on protein baits, milk protein bait and HNV's back in the late seventies;

they were, and still are, brilliant baits and if I was ever in a position to fish waters like I was fishing in those days, waters that had never seen an HNV before I would use them again. Today I try to be different from other anglers and if most people are on HNV's, I go in with bird foods and the results are clear. Now I'm seeing more and more people on bird foods so perhaps I'll have to change to, say, fishmeals, but if everyone is on the fish I may even revert to protein baits. If you change the nature of the bait by making it a high fat diet with the aid of an oil soak you can give any bait a whole new lease of life by changing such things as flavours, smells and taste. We all know that sweet baits were excellent and the change to spice has been almost as good, so perhaps we will be looking at a more salty taste in the future or even something acidic like vinegar. I know some of my mates have done well on soya sauce and hoisin black bean sauces. They are quite salty and can change the identity of a bait.

Crap baits is a name that I don't really comprehend. Cheap baits, made with cheaper ingredients, have always been a favourite of mine and a good bird food can be made simply by adding equal quantities of nectablend and semolina, and mark my words if this sort of bait hasn't been widely used on your waters it can be devastating. The big advantage with this sort of bait and with particles is that they don't fill them up, they can keep on feeding and this will increase your chances of a bite.

All this talk of long term and short term baits is rubbish in my opinion, relative to the big fish waters I am fishing. You just don't stand a chance as everyone is chucking in something different, and the trouble is with the quality of angler on these waters they are all bloody good baits. The carp could well be eating some of everyone's so it's just impossible to get a bait established that's so different and so much better than everyone else is using, so you might as well use a cheap bait. On the other hand some of the ingredients that are very attractive to the fish are not cheap, so you may formulate a cheap base mix with more expensive appetite stimulators and fish feed inducers and that's what puts the cost up.

So I haven't changed my mind on baits and in my range of baits are some cheap and some expensive ones. You have to cover the whole spectrum of baits so as to appeal to the majority. My thoughts are that if you're going in on a new water almost anything will catch fish but HNV's could well be your best bet. If you're fishing a water where everyone's chucking in good quality baits of all different types, you may as well use one of the cheaper mixes but with a good quality bait soak and flavour, and finally if you are still confused as to what sort of bait to use remember the golden rule of being different, not only with the base mix but also colour and size of bait as well.

Question—I've been looking at a water with a couple of mates for a while now. It's not really carp fished but a couple of blokes told us there were some really big ones in there. It's quite large and some of the other lakes nearby have got good carp in them. We haven't actually seen any fish in there ourselves. How should we go about fishing it?

Answer—Don't waste your time! That's my first response to this sort of question, and believe me this one comes up a lot. Unless you actually see the fish, see photos or know someone 'well' who has actually caught fish there and is willing to show you the photos, I wouldn't fish it. I've walked around dozens of lakes in the close season that I was sure contained big fish. I just couldn't understand how a lake down the road could contain many big fish and this one not, but it's rare to find a new 'Savay' these days with so many people in the game.

When I say don't waste your time, I don't mean don't waste some time in the close season looking. In fact I would spend every available minute looking around in the close season. Especially on hot calm days, they just can't resist getting up on the surface in these conditions so you should be able to see something. Look in the snag trees, in beds of pad, and get a boat out if it's allowed. Put out plenty of Mixers; if you spend enough time on the water you should see them if they are there. If you don't see anything my advice is to keep an eye on the water by all means but go on a water with known big fish. There are still plenty of waters where the full potential of the water has not been exploited but it is known to have definitely produced some big kippers in the past.

Rigs

This chapter will combine all of the terminal rigs I have used and helped develop over the past eight years. All of these rigs will still catch today but some are more suitable for certain types of fishing than others and an explanation of the use of each rig taken from my first two books *Tiger Bay* and *Fox Pool* should help you decide what rig is best suited to the type of water you are fishing.

Rigs are very fashionable, they change with the times and these days there is a great trend towards the use of the bent hook. You will find a couple of variations later in this section, but don't forget some of the other rigs which still are very effective. Buoyant hooks in particular have a lot more scope. We're all too eager to jump on the bandwagon when a new rig hits the headlines but don't let us forget the basics because one day we may all be freelining again!

As you will see the diagrams and text have been taken from the aforementioned publications, which are the two most up-to-date accounts of rigs and although there are a couple of new rigs in the pipeline I am not at liberty to divulge this information at present. So what you are really getting is two books for the price of one. 'The how to catch them' and the 'Advanced Terminal Rig book'. Think about the water and the education of the fish before you decide on what rig to use, it could make the world of difference.

Critical Balancing

If a buoyant bait can be weighted so that it just sinks it will do a series of things; it will rest upon silt or weed, it will overcome its restriction to movement caused by a heavy hook or line stiffness, it can waft up enticingly when affected by any water displacement in its vicinity, such as vortices caused by a moving carp; it will, if surrounded by other heavier baits, be the first to be sucked into the carp's mouth even if the suck is not aimed directly at that particular area but it falls within the volume of water consumed by the carp, and very importantly because of its extreme buoyancy it resists the carp's natural reaction to regulate 'suck' upon a food item that it is unsure of. Thus it makes it difficult for the bait to be sucked gently up and held between the lips and inspected, as is the case on many hard fished waters these days. Only a slight suck causes the bait to be drawn rapidly into the carp's throat and this in itself causes instant fright to the carp. It now realises the bait has behaved unnaturally but unfortunately it's a bit late now as the hook is inside the fishes' mouth; it has but two choices, to try to rid itself of the offending item, or bolt. Its natural reaction a couple of seasons ago would be to bolt thus giving those unmissable roaring runs, but today, due to the conditioning we have given the carp, it resists this urge and on many occasions tries to eject the bait if possible as it realises from past experience that to bolt now means a session before the camera—and we all know how camera shy most carp are. Some, however, seem to take every opportunity to pose for the weeklies; perhaps these are the exhibitionists of the carp world.

Anyway, back to this carp with the hook and bait in its mouth. As yet it may not actually be hooked, in which case it still could blow out the bait. That's where the anti-eject baits and rigs described later in the chapter come into their own. There is, however, a critical line between success and—well, not total failure, but let's say the excellent results which can be obtained with precise balancing. If the bait is not balanced as near perfectly as possible (say you test your bait in the margins and you think maybe it's sinking a bit fast but it's close enough), you may then give the fish the chance it needs to recognise and reject the unnatural offering. If that bait is not spot on, remembering that in time the bait will take on water and become less and less effective, so it will not rocket straight to the back of the throat of the carp. No chance to inspect the bait with the lips must be given as the bait will undoubtedly feel different from your ground baits and if the fish decides to back off with the bait held between its lips the length of the hook link can restrict its movement. This too can be overcome by using the extending hook link rigs shown later in this chapter. The hook rejection system which is now used by carp of many waters cannot be ignored and it is indeed a valuable weapon for the carp.

I will relate to you an incident which occurred while fishing a London reservoir several seasons ago. During the day several hook baits had dropped into the margin, during the baiting up and discarding of baits, until about a dozen could be seen on the near margin in about two feet of water. Action had been slow and when a mirror of about 6lb entered the swim along the shelf it was too great an opportunity to miss. A rod was quickly reeled in and as the fish moved off slowly into the deeper water beyond the shelf, a few more freebies and a hookbait attached to a 3oz lead on a 6 inch hooklink was lowered amongst them. The carp had upended and consumed about six of the old baits and could well return for seconds. Sure enough 15 minutes later it came back in the swim, took two more free ones and then upended on the hookbait. It swallowed the bait which was attached to the hair on a size 6 hook. My first reaction was to give it the butt and send it screaming off into the lake, but I resisted the temptation and this is what I observed. The carp began to shake its head violently from side to side, then it rotated its whole body about the line; still it hadn't taken an inch of line from me and no actual movement other than a slight knocking could be seen along the line. Then it blew the bait out, 'sat up' squarely in the water and swam casually off. I stood there with my mouth hanging open. Then I began to laugh. It had got away with it, the little bastard had actually done it. Then the hard reality really hit me. How often was this happening out there in the lake and while I was sitting here thinking they're not taking the bait when all the time they're clearing up my free offerings like there's no tomorrow. Now I'm not silly enough to believe they all get away with it, but you don't need many fish to do it to turn a season's results from good to bad.

It was time to get back to the drawing board and as I'm a design draughtsman anyway it wasn't too difficult. These are my observations and my opinion drawn from them. I may be totally wrong, but this is what I think and it may spark off a similar line of thought in people of a like mind. So that's basically the theory, now I'll describe what equipment I have used to achieve the best results; there may be better ways but here are my suggestions.

I never use split shot directly pinched onto the hooklink; a bad experience with a big fish which parted the line at the shot has caused me to re-think the weighting device. I came up with the idea of putting a 5mm length of silicon tube, as used for float rubbers, on the hook link Into this I push a small piece of lead wire; it's a similar principle to the old fashioned leger stops, only a lead weight is used as the insert. This weight alone should not sink the hook bait but with the addition of a small piece of lead substitute putty, such as that under the name of Evode Anglers Weight, moulded around the rubber stop, a perfect sink rate can be obtained. Simply pull off tiny pieces until the bait just sinks and remember if you're using braided terylene links, these should be wetted before testing the buoyancy as the added weight due to absorption can make a slight difference.

The majority of my carp fishing over the past ten years has been with the use of boilies. I have always felt confidence in my own bait and even when fishing particles preferred to use a boilie over the top. A few years ago, however, when peanuts were going very well in the south, I came to the conclusion that equally good if not better results could be achieved by using the same particle with a little modification to its buoyancy over the bed. This was further verified when I met Dick

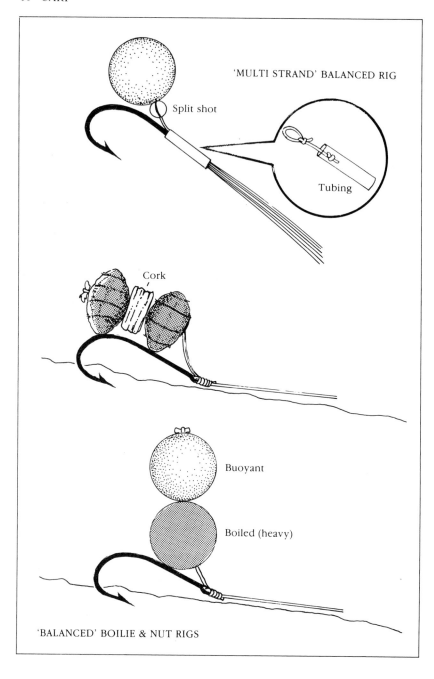

'MULTI STRAND' BALANCED RIG

Split shot

Tubing

Cork

Buoyant

Boiled (heavy)

'BALANCED' BOILIE & NUT RIGS

Caldwell several seasons ago when he was doing well with 'tigers' at Savay; he confirmed my findings and agreed that he too had achieved better results with actually fishing tigers on the hook. Therefore a couple of buoyant particle rigs were developed and it is these which I shall describe first. These were developed for use with nuts but would obviously work with any particles.

Balanced Nut

As already emphasised my preference is to fish nuts over nuts as opposed to a different hook bait, though in the past I have experienced a good response by fishing boilies, luncheon meat or even a different particle over the loose feed. If, however, I am using 'tigers' or peanuts, by far the best results have come by using the same hook bait, but in a buoyant or balanced manner. Balanced presentation requires no additional weight on the line. A small piece of cork resembling the size and shape of the nut is positioned alongside one or more nuts on the hair. I prefer to fish one nut either side of the cork. The cork and the nuts can then be trimmed with a pair of nail clippers until the whole lot just sinks. When this rig is presented amongst a bed of similar items it will rise rapidly from the bottom when sucked. I recommend the 'through the eye' method of hair-rigging when using particles, although a rotating hair can be a useful alternative.

Normally the carp are so engrossed in consuming the tiny items that all investigation of the particles is abandoned.

Buoyant Nut

The buoyant nut presentation can prove very effective when fishing over rotting vegetation or thick silt, as it has the advantage of stacking the bait above the hook. When fishing in normal conditions, however, I have found a balance presentation usually outfishes the stack method. Cork or polystyrene is used as the buoyancy aid once again, though this time the bait is made over-buoyant, so that an additional weight needs to be added to the line, below the hook, to hold the bait down. The weight should be critically balanced as described earlier in the chapter.

Before moving onto other rig designs, hook link materials suitable for link manufacture must be fully understood. Carp anglers have always strived towards supple materials, as nylon line stiffness was observed in tank tests to offer great resistance to feeding carp. The more supple and free moving the link material the more natural the bait moves in the water. The natural progression from nylon lines to braided links was made many years ago and basically that's where the progression stopped. Without doubt these new man-made braided cords are very effective with

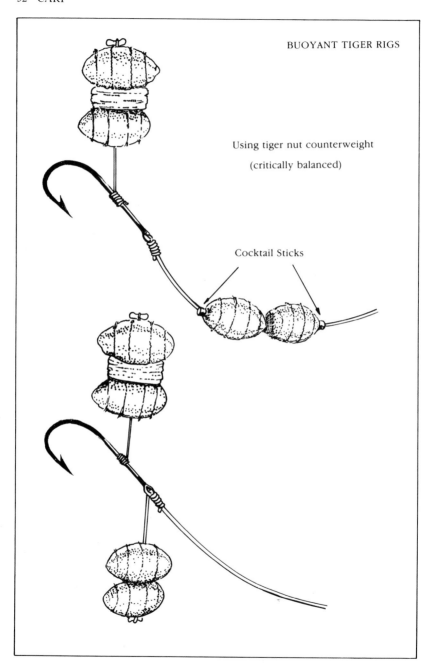

BUOYANT TIGER RIGS

Using tiger nut counterweight

(critically balanced)

Cocktail Sticks

more and more supple alternatives. The two brands I have found very effective are, firstly CORTLAND MICRON, a very fine white braid, which can be purchased in tournament casting grade in strains of 15 and 20 pound BS; this make I find very good in all but snag fishing as its abrasion resistance is not as good as MILLWARDS MEDIUM FLYLINE BACKING, this being the other braid I use. I use the 30 pound breaking strain, straight through, for snag fishing, especially where hook-and-hold tactics are necessary. It has larger diameter than the micron but is very supple and has no stretch, which is useful when fish are to be restrained from entering snags. They are both white but can be dyed easily with a permanent marker pen.

If you look closely at braided lines you will see they are composed of may fine lines woven together; it was this idea which formed the basis behind out next hook link design, 'the multi-strand link'. As, the title suggests, it is made up of several fine strands, but instead of being braided together they are separate. One pound nylon is an obvious choice for the strands. Cut off eight strands at about the same length, approximately eight inches long, wet the ends and tie the lot to the hook; the rig is then completed with a swivel at the other end. The breaking strain is now approximately eight times one pound, but the suppleness far exceeds that of eight pound nylon line. The only disadvantage I have found with this link is its abrasion resistance which is poor. However with short hook links this is less of a problem.

The final material I have used with success is dental floss, the unwaxed unflavoured type being best. This, too, comprises many fine strands but is by far the most supple, though least abrasion resistant. I usually renew hook lines after every fish as it tends to fray. Today's modern braids such as Gamabraid, Kryston Merlin and Kryston Silkworm are also good alternatives.

Now we have looked at the link materials we can move on to the types of rig most suitable for modern day carp angling.

Through-The-Eye

The standard through-the-eye hair rig is a very efficient exposed hook rig and providing the distances between bait and the bend of the hook is kept at a minimum, it has many of the properties of the anti-eject-rigs, in that, as the bait is sucked up, the hook goes in bend first but as the bait is blown out, the action of the bait pulling against the eye ensures that the point faces outward on rejection. This rig is simple to tie for both buoyant and non-buoyant presentations; simply tie the hook in the normal way leaving the loose end about three inches long, then pass this end back through the eye towards to back of the shank and tie a small loop on the end so that when the bait is pulled onto the looped

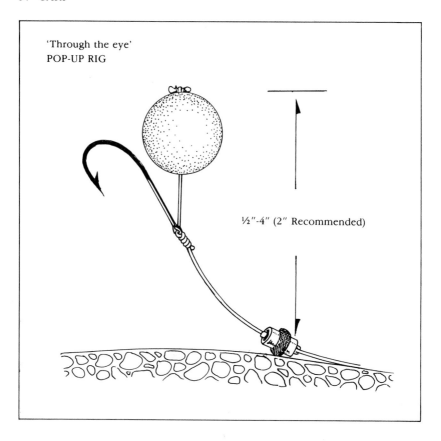

'Through the eye'
POP-UP RIG

½"-4" (2" Recommended)

end, the outside of the bait is close to the bend of the hook. This distance can be determined only by trial and error as it depends on the size of the boilie you are using.

Revolving Hair Rig

This rig is really only efficient with buoyant baits as the bait must be kept close to the hook. The principle behind this rig is as follows. The bait is attached to a piece of line which is equal to the length of the hook, plus the diameter of the bait. To one end of this piece of line is tied a loop to fix to the boilie, to the other a small ring or bead which has an internal diameter smaller than the eye of the hook, but large enough to slide freely on the hook link. The rig is assembled as follows: tie the hook on one end of the hook line, slide the small ring down the link

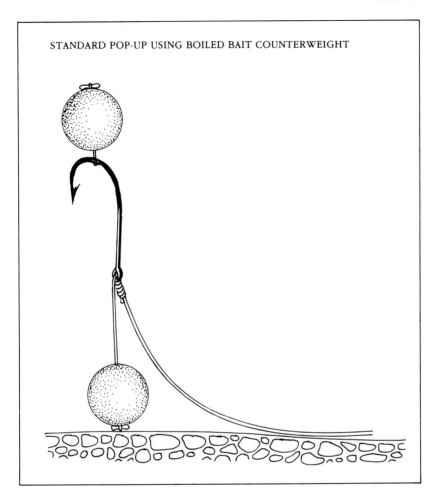

STANDARD POP-UP USING BOILED BAIT COUNTERWEIGHT

then affix the weight; decide what length you require the link to be which I would suggest is somewhere between 8–12 inches.

As you can see when the bait is attached to the hair link the small ring can move between the eye of the hook and the weight. If you are using the critical weight method the weight is adjusted until it just sinks. You will see that when the rig sits on the bottom, the buoyant bait pulls the ring up to rest against the eye of the hook. The trap is now set. When sucked up by the carp, the hook and bait all go up together, but if the fish decides to blow the bait out the large buoyant bait slides down the line leaving the small but comparatively heavy hook within the mouth.

THE 'REVOLVING' HAIR RIG

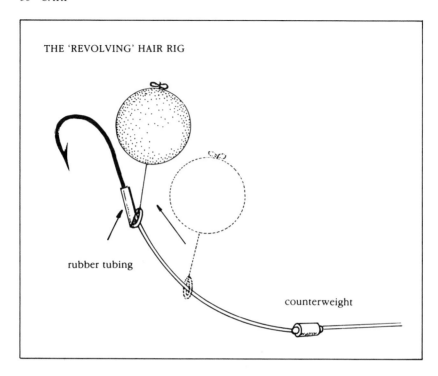

rubber tubing

counterweight

This is probably enough to prick the fish, but, as an added bonus, as the ring hits the weight it gives a little jerk on the hook just to push it home. Now slight modifications can be made to improve this rig. A small piece of anti-tangle tube can be pushed over the eye of the hook and cut off at a 45 degree angle as in diagram. The line then slides up behind this angled section and makes the hook sit correctly. When using braided hooklinks, the section of link between the eye and the weight can be varnished; this effectively provides an extension to the hook shank and a friction resistant surface for the ring to slide on.

Sliding or Tandem Hooklink Rig

This particular rig was specifically designed for very wary fish on hard fished waters. Perhaps before I describe this rig, a little of the background to its development may help you to determine when this type of rig is necessary.

When the hair rig and its early variations first hit the hard fished waters of the country the fish took a severe hammering. Many fish which

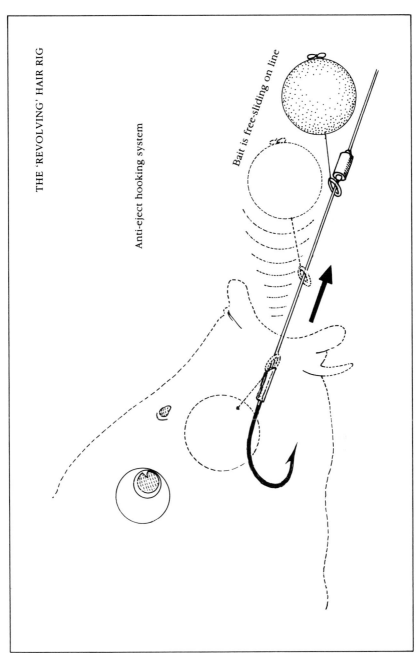

THE 'REVOLVING' HAIR RIG

Anti-eject hooking system

Bait is free-sliding on line

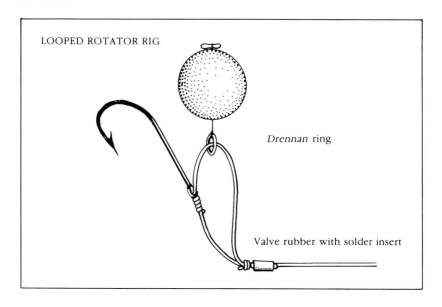

LOOPED ROTATOR RIG

Drennan ring

Valve rubber with solder insert

were thought to be virtually uncatchable were now being caught several times a season. It was truly a birthday for the carp angler; unfortunately, it was to have an equally devastating effect on the carp. Baits which the carp felt totally safe eating were proving not to be so, and gradually this 'slaughter' was going to take its toll. You see, carp are only as educated as we make them. Gradually they began to wise up to the hair. Thus improvements on the basic hair rig became necessary. Rod Hutchinson was probably one of the first to experiment and his extending hair rig gave him the edge over his fellow Savay Syndicate members. Since then the number of variations has escalated, I'm sure past any expectations Kevin Maddocks and Len Middleton may have had years ago, so when on certain waters a couple of seasons ago anglers began to experience dropped takes, rod top knocking and fish which were only hooked at the very edge of the mouth, it was obvious that the carp were treating all baits with a lot more suspicion. Because of the short hooklinks and tight lines so popular at this time the carp realised that even if at first inspection the food item appeared totally safe, if it picked it up carefully in the lips and slowly backed off, the bait would be restricted in its move-ment, due to the length of the hooklink. Some anglers began to use very long tail confidence rigs which by bunching the link up and tying with PVA could be cast a fair distance. Although this method solved the prob-lem to a degree, by giving them enough rope to hang themselves, if you like, it was inefficient and inclined to tangle. The carp obviously needed

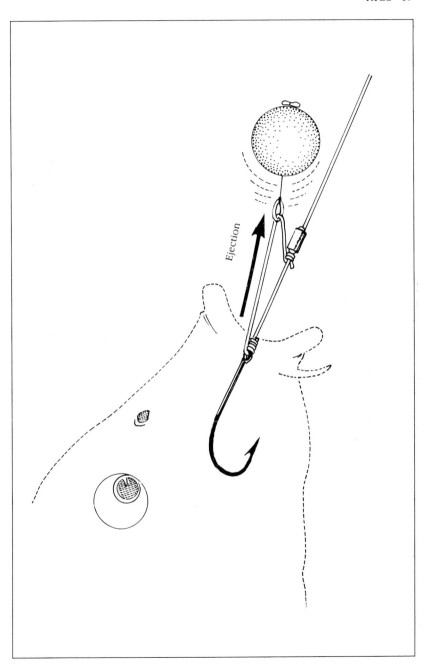

Ejection

to move away from the point where they picked the bait up before they were willing to swallow it back to the throat teeth.

The answer was obvious, either make the bait so light it was difficult for the fish to manoeuvre it carefully to the lips, (critical balancing) or improve upon the extending hooklink rig. The sliding or tandem hooklink provides a temporary solution to the problem; I say temporary because rig development and the carp education to these developments is an on-going thing. Another advantage of this rig is that no matter what direction the carp decides to suck from, the bait comes to the fish. This means that unlike conventional fixed length rigs which can be movement restric-tive if sucked when the rig is at full length on the bottom, this rig still comes to the fish whichever way it is sucked. The rig is tied like this; first attach the hook to one end of a piece of line leaving enough tail for a loop. Cut this first length of line at about 18 inches. Then take another 18 inches of line and tie a Drennan ring to one end, slide a second Drennan ring onto the link and finally tie a swivel to the other end. Then taking the first link, pass the free end through the fixed Drennan rig and tie it to the running Drennan ring. The two links now slide parallel to each other. The sliding ring is then PVA'd to the swivel for casting. As the fish sucks at the bait the sliding ring can slide down the link until it meets the fixed ring, effectively giving you a tangle free link of three feet. The rig has proved very effective during the winter months when fish may prove to be a bit more finicky than normal.

Stack Baits

This rig is fairly straightforward being similar to through-the-eye hair rigging, but offering a visual aid in that it is different and sticks out. This rig can be very effective if a string of boilies is used. The only reason I can see that it is so effective is simply that it is different from the other free offerings and maybe attractive standing up from the bottom or through a layer of silt.

Fine Line Links

A lot of emphasis these days falls upon the effect line stiffness has upon the movement of the bait. Obviously the finer the line, the more freedom of movement, but the obvious drawback is that you lose line strength; so was born the 'shock resistant' light line rig. Quite simply, it is a length of fine line attached to a similar length of match fisherman's power gum, a shock resistant plastic line which is used on match anglers' roach poles to prevent snap-off on light lines. The power gum can be found in various diameters and breaking strains, the one which breaks around 15lb being the most suitable. I would not advise this rig to be

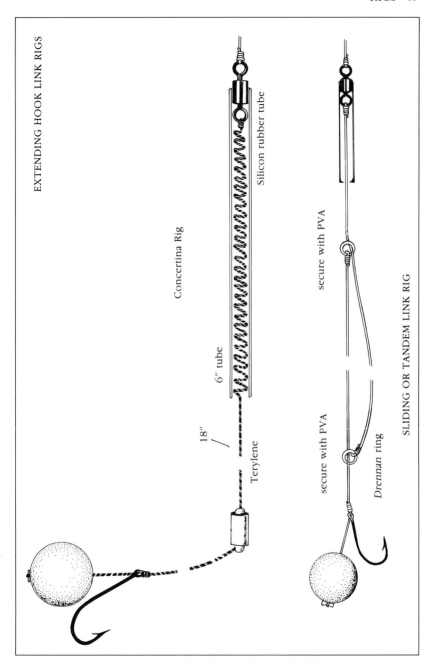

EXTENDING HOOK LINK RIGS

Concertina Rig

Silicon rubber tube

6″ tube

18″

Terylene

secure with PVA

secure with PVA

Drennan ring

SLIDING OR TANDEM LINK RIG

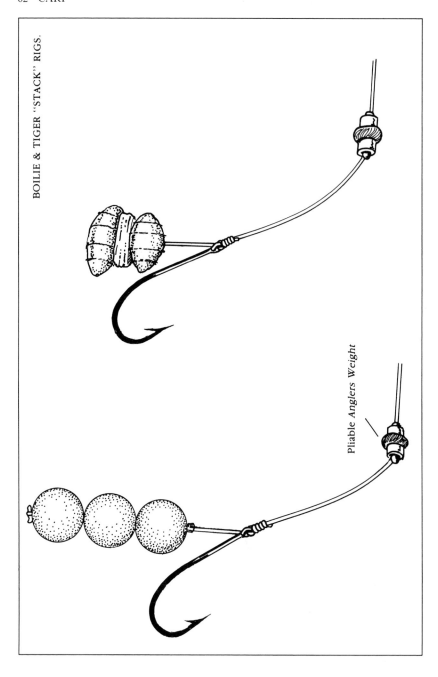

BOILIE & TIGER "STACK" RIGS.

Pliable Anglers Weight

SHOCK RESISTANT "FINE LINK" RIG

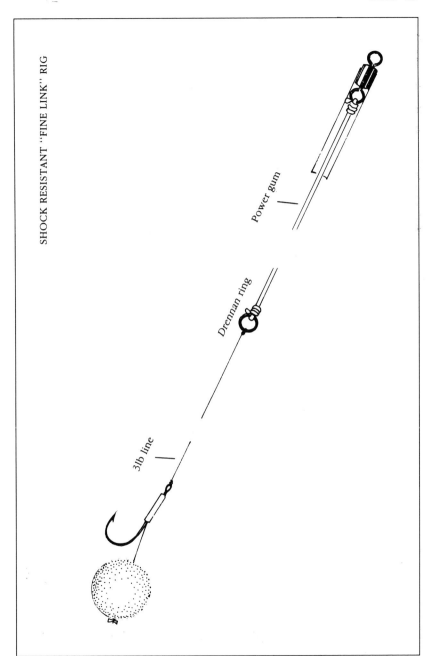

Power gum

Drennan ring

3lb line

used in waters which have any snags, and that rather cuts down its effectiveness, I think. Many anglers adopted this rig at its concept and without doubt received a good response. However, the overall percentage of losses far exceeded the gain in takes and most have now ceased to use this rig, except on snag free lakes where the accepted size of the fish would not be too large.

Concertina Extending Link

This particular rig is still in development though I do know of several fish taken from Harefield on it. I have not used it though I can see possibilities. The link material must be braided as you will see when I describe it. Tie a hook to the end of a 15″ length of terylene and slide a six inch length of thin silicon tube onto it, then tie a swivel to the other end and push the end of the tube halfway up the swivel, so it is fixed in place. Now stretch the tube down to the hook and allow it to retract slowly, gathering up the terylene braid as it retracts, with a concertina effect. This reduces the hooklink to about ten inches. Care in casting is necessary as well as a light bait, but medium range particle fishing is well suited. As the fish pulls on the bait the line extends giving the carp extra distance to move off the bait and the confidence to swallow the bait.

The sliding Pop-up Rig

The bait is simply slid up the line before the hook is tied on. If, however, the pop-ups are made without a hole, the careful insertion of a small length of biro-tube can be as effective. The buoyancy of the bait pulls the small hook up above the bait and when critically balanced both will enter the mouth rapidly. If the carp then tries to reject the bait, it slides up the line to the balance weight which can either be a lead substitute weight or a heavy boilie which is held in position between two leger stops.

I have found it most effective with smallish hooks, as large heavy hooks tend to sag above the bait. The few people that I have divulged this presentation to have been using hooks as small as size 10 on most waters; as long as the hook is strong you should still be able to achieve a good hook hold and most have said the hardest part is getting the hooks out once they're in. Give it a try. I used this rig at a small day ticket water called Stanborough about ten years ago and had incredible results.

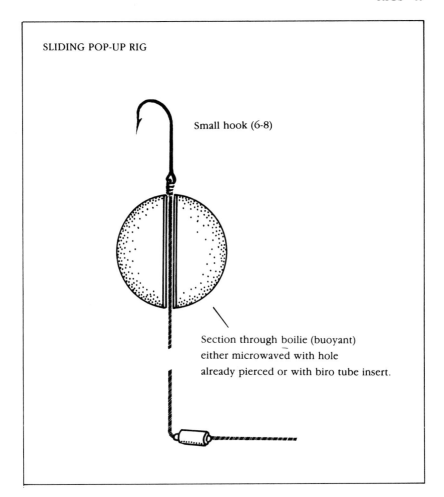

SLIDING POP-UP RIG

Small hook (6-8)

Section through boilie (buoyant)
either microwaved with hole
already pierced or with biro tube insert.

Buoyant Hook Rig

The buoyant hook presentation is certainly controversial at the moment as many feel that far too many carp are being foul hooked. I've used this method for six seasons and with a little thought behind the way in which it should be used have come up with a rig which has only ever caused me to foul hook one fish, and even then only just outside the mouth. The problem is that many anglers are using the rig with heavy non-buoyant hook baits and I think this is where the problem is occurring. The fish are still being allowed to mouth the bait in the extremities of

SLIDING POP-UP RIG

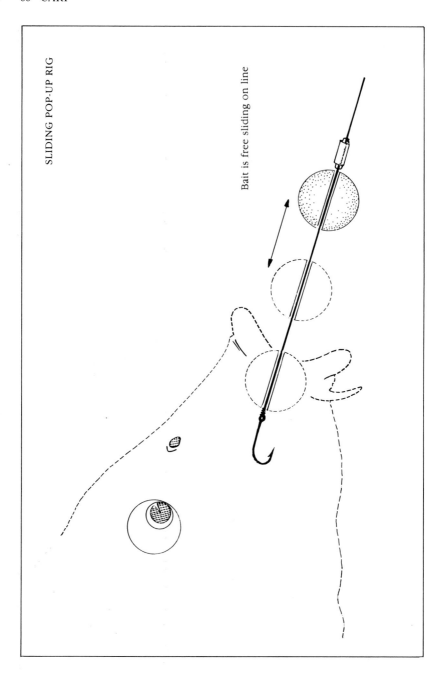

Bait is free sliding on line

the lips; in theory the light hook should always enter the mouth first, but in practice it doesn't. The heavy boilie allows suck to be regulated upon it and the bait is drawn quite slowly from the bottom. It has been shown in tank tests that the hook can catch on the outside of the mouth unless the distance from hook to bait is quite long, say over three inches. If a critically balanced bait is used below the buoyant hook, as the fish sucks, the whole lot shoots to the throat before it has a chance to mouth it. The hook and bait go in very quickly and together. The hook, which should be small and as always, very sharp, is then free to swirl around inside the carp's mouth where it catches on the soft tissue inside the mouth. It is quite common to hook fish well back in the mouth when using this presentation. The bait can either be a double balanced arrangement or a single bait off the bottom with a hook above it. Alternatively if the weight is placed directly behind the boilie the rig will sit nicely on the bottom with the hook hovering about it. This rig will without doubt be the cornerstone of many variations around future buoyancy rigs.

The Looney Extension

This particular rig invented by several members of the 'Looney Rota' on Redlands Savay Lake, was arrived at as the solution to a different problem from 'suck regulation' although it soon became apparent after its inception that 'critical balancing' and the extension were far more efficient when used together. The extension came about after I passed a theory of mine on to Martin Locke about the position of the hook relative to the bait. It was my opinion that because the hook was below the bait the unconverted takes we were receiving were due to the bait being taken but not the hook. Instead of the bait being sucked up, the carp were going down and taking the bait within their lips, and because the bait was above the hook they weren't getting it. It was also my opinion that sometimes, after the carp realised something was wrong, it clamped up on the bait instead of ejecting it, and belted off up the lake, hence the screamer that had absolutely nothing on the end when you pick the rod up. Sometimes you actually feel a bump, it could be that the hook has only nicked into some very soft tissue, or it could be that you are pulling the bait out of its mouth. I've pulled floaters out of carp's mouths before, so perhaps it's even possible with bottom baits, especially if the hook isn't set!

The method and equipment I describe to tie in all these rigs is purely personal. They are the best I have found for the job but you pays yer money and you takes your choice.

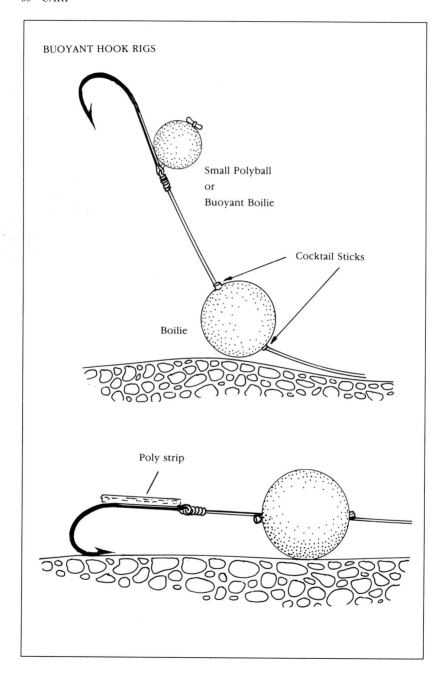

BUOYANT HOOK RIGS

Small Polyball
or
Buoyant Boilie

Cocktail Sticks

Boilie

Poly strip

DENTAL FLOSS POP-UP METHOD

Apparatus

Size 6 O'Shaunessey (MUSTAD), 25mm of 1mm Nashy Rig Tube, small loop of nylon about 5mm long, Gardener baiting needle, and

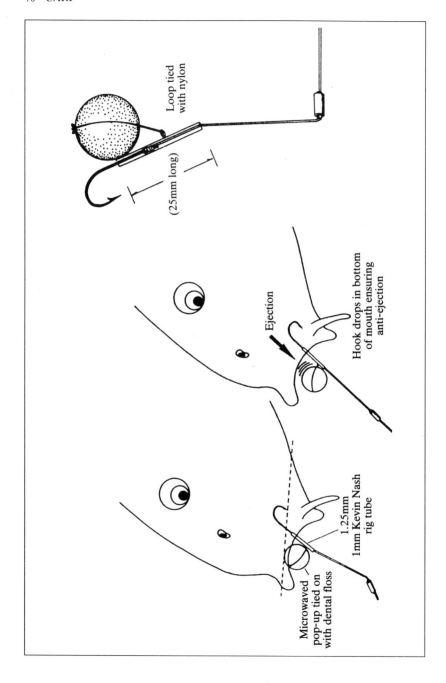

Loop tied
with nylon

(25mm long)

Ejection

Hook drops in bottom
of mouth ensuring
anti-ejection

1.25mm
1mm Kevin Nash
rig tube

Microwaved
pop-up tied on
with dental floss

obviously hook link material; I'm using 15lb camouflaged-braided nylon, and a weight to anchor the pop-up (a piece of lead wire 5mm long pushed into 5mm of 1mm dia silicon tube), critically weighted with the addition of tungsten putty, and finally a Berkley swivel.

Method

Tie the hook to one end of the braid, push the rig tube down and force the end over the eye of the hook and slide the small nylon loop down to the rig tube. Now push the baiting needle into the side of the rig tube about 10mm from the end and push the needle out through the end of the rig tube, hook the nylon loop onto the needle and pull the loop into the end of the rig tube and out of the side of the rig tube; the knot in the loop remains inside the rig tube. Slide the silicon tube down and push the lead wire into it to hold in position, about two inches from the end of the rig tube. The tungsten putty will stick to the silicon tube for 'critical balancing'. Cut the braid off at about nine to ten inches and tie on the swivel. The pop-up is then simply tied to the small nylon loop by the dental floss. Easy, almost guaranteed a thirty every time you use it!

The Sliding Extension

A modification to the looney extension, the initial concept for this rig was originally designed by that brilliant Harefield angler, Tony More, from Coventry. This rig works similarly to the extension in that the hook is pushed up higher in relation to the bait but also has the added advantage of good anti-ejection properties. Basically the apparatus needed for this rig is the same as for the extension, only a small brass Drennan ring is needed as an extra.

Method

The 25mm length of 1.5mm diameter Kevin Nash rig tube is cut away in a 'C' section as shown in the diagram. The rig is tied by first tying the hook, then passing the loose end of the hook link through one end of the hook link through one end of the rig tube and out through the slot, then pass the loose end of the hook link through the Drennan ring, then back into the slot and out of the other end of the rig tube. Now force the end of the rig tube over the eye of the hook. The ring now slides on the line, held within the raised ends of the 'C' section slot. Finish the rig as per the extension and tie off at about nine to ten inches. The bait is then tied to the Drennan ring using dental floss. Although

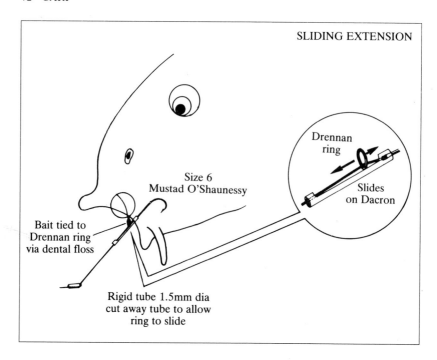

SLIDING EXTENSION

Drennan
ring

Slides
on Dacron

Size 6
Mustad O'Shaunessy

Bait tied to
Drennan ring
via dental floss

Rigid tube 1.5mm dia
cut away tube to allow
ring to slide

rig tubing is stiff enough for most people who use this rig, I have had better results using a slightly stiffer tube, e.g. biro tubing.

The Swimmer Rig

This rig was probably the most effective rig used by anglers I know fishing the Colne Valley in recent years; quite why it is so effective I'm afraid I am unsure. At a casual glance one can see no real advantage over a conventional 'eye-tied hair' but try telling some of the anglers who have experienced terrific action using this rig, including its inventor Roger Smith. Dave Whibley used this rig to the exclusion of all others at Fox Pool in 1988, and included in this impressive list of big fish taken on this rig were fish of 41lb 12oz and 35lb 14oz. I have sat and studied this rig on many occasions looking for its secret and the only thing I have come up with is the angle at which the hook sits to the bait. The nylon braid is super-glued to stand at right angles to the hook shank and because the Kamatsu hook is so light combined with its needle sharpness all go to enhance the effectiveness of the rig. The rig also accounted for many of the big fish taken by the Famous Five and the 40lb 8oz common taken by Zenon Bojko, so action speaks louder than words; whatever it is, this rig certainly does the business.

Method

The rig itself is pretty straightforward so I won't bother to go all through it. One little tip I can give you however, concerns the making of the little loop which you push back through the eye and super-glue. I always tie the little loop first on the end of the dacron. The loop should be about 5mm long, then pass the other end of the hook link through the hook eye and tie your knot using the little loop as one end of the line. When you tighten the knot it is possible to pull this little loop standing proud down by the hook eye. The bait can be tied on at this point giving an unusual angle to the hook, or you can pull the little loop back through the eye using a piece of fine line, then simply dab the loop with glue and blow it to clear the hole; the bait is tied on using dental floss. Incidentally it was several German anglers on Lake Cassien that christened it the 'Swimmer' rig. Swimmers are simply the name they give to pop-ups, in other words they swim above the bottom, so really this rig is simply what the Germans call their pop-up rig. They've kept pretty quiet about it so far but 've have vays of making zem talk'.

Power Gums Rigs (Update)

Since the introduction of the power gum shock rigs several years ago, I've been looking at the spool of gum I bought wondering what I was going to do with it. The shock rigs were destined to be short lived because of the increased losses due to the light line either snapping or chafing on a snag, so many people were left with a spool of something which really didn't seem to have a use. Stop knots to fix leads can be tied with it, as it does tend to be kinder to the main line than tying a stop knot with ordinary nylon line, but its real advantage lies in its ability to stretch and retract rather than its shock absorbing properties.

Side-mounted or eye-mounted boilies were always a problem to tie dead tight to the hook as most people who have tried these two rigs would agree, however, using a small loop of power gum tied or whipped to the shank or the eye solves the problem. The loop should be no longer than half of the diameter of the boilie, then simply push the boilie onto a Gardener baiting needle and hook the power gum loop onto the needle barb, pull the gum through the bait under tension and slide on a small stop. The bait is then pulled tight to the shank or eye.

The exploding stringer is based on the same idea. This time, however, the small loop is pulled through several baits under maximum tension and a small piece of Alka Seltzer is placed under the loop once through

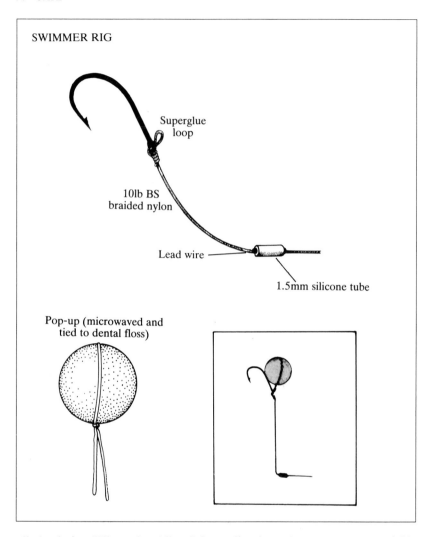

SWIMMER RIG

Superglue loop

10lb BS braided nylon

Lead wire

1.5mm silicone tube

Pop-up (microwaved and tied to dental floss)

all the baits. When the Alka Seltzer dissolves the power gum quickly returns to its original size, freeing the baits and disturbing their pattern. The small loop for this rig can either be tied to the swivel on the bomb or to the hook as long as penetration is not obscured.

Bent Hook Rig

This one is the kiddy, folks, absolutely the business! Quite where it originated is hard to pin-point. Many of the 'Longfield Drinking Team'

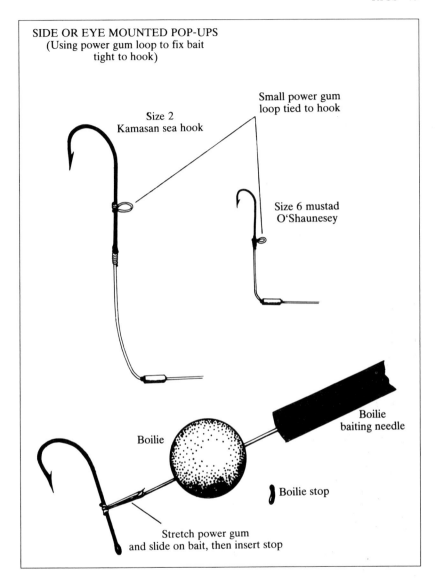

SIDE OR EYE MOUNTED POP-UPS
(Using power gum loop to fix bait
tight to hook)

Small power gum
loop tied to hook

Size 2
Kamasan sea hook

Size 6 mustad
O'Shaunesey

Boilie

Boilie
baiting needle

Boilie stop

Stretch power gum
and slide on bait, then insert stop

would place its birth in the hands of 'Secret John'. I'm not sure if one man invented it or it was reached by several groups of anglers around the same time. I know the idea is not new by any means; Lenny Middleton experimented with bending hooks way back in the early eighties when he was fishing with Kevin Maddocks, but I'm sure that even he couldn't have realised its potential or why it works so well.

Why does it work? What do I mean? Right, let me take you back to Savay in the summer of 1985. I sat in the snag tree watching three carp, all very large, and all with their heads down on a few handfuls of boilies I had thrown out under the sticks, probably the most inaccessible spot on the whole lake to put a bait. One would assume then it would also be one of the safest. The carp had visited the baits three times since I threw them in a little over an hour ago. They were very suspicious, but there again they always were. Eventually they began to feed, taking one bait at a time, slowly and then munching it up. At a casual glance it looked as if they were having it, even if cautiously having it. Then I noticed something they were doing, something very subtle. They were backing off slightly with each bait as they took it, fanning their pectorals to push themselves backward, only an inch or so most of the time, but every now and again several inches. I couldn't really see if the bait was in the lips or in the mouth. At the time I thought they must have been holding the bait lightly in their lips, then backing off, their super-sensitive receptors around the mouth and barbules testing for any resistance. It looked, at first glance as if they were just taking the bait and looking round for another, but it was more than that, they were actually testing each one with practised ease.

As I said at the time I thought the baits were in the lips but further observation at Fox Pool in 1988 has led me to think the baits were actually in the mouth! When they were backing off they were actually feeling for the line pulling over the lips or rim of the mouth as they moved away. Why weren't we hooking all these fish then if they had the hook and bait in their mouths? Well, because they could still eject it, that is why. They could still blow it out. The hook just didn't take hold. Back then to '85; on the strength of what I had seen I began to look at ways of allowing them to back off without pulling on the line. Extending hook links and the concertina rig shown earlier, brought results, so I thought that was the answer.

Those same rigs didn't work on Fox Pool, but observation in the safe areas showed they were still backing off. Now I'm not suggesting for one minute that all carp in all lakes feed or behave the same; they don't and that's a fact, but the carp on these two lakes, which we already knew were hyper-sensitive and very cautious, definitely were doing it. Not all the time, but sometimes. I was so blind I just couldn't see what I needed to do, and in time what with everything else to think about, it was put to the back of my mind. That was until one day Clive Williams showed me something and the penny dropped. He had been using the bent hook to great effect wherever he fished from easier lakes like Broadlands in Hampshire to Fox Pool, certainly the hardest place I had ever

A 29-0 Springwood lump.

Yateley whacker; 30-04.

A long Savay fish caught on particle boilies.

The North Lake at Yateley.

Look at the rudder on this one!

Springwood Lake.

The best feeling in carp fishing.

32-12 – North Bay pads, October 1985.

The 'Torpedo'.

Returning a Springwood 31-12.

Poplar's mid-twenty, June 1989.

Kent twenty.

Sit back and dream . . . .

fished, and his results were conclusive; he was out-catching everyone wherever he went. Clive showed me his rig, then did something very interesting with it, he draped the hook link over his finger, as in the drawing, and slowly pulled it up his finger. The hook flipped round as it reached his finger and dug in. So what's the significance of that? No other rig I was using did this. It was caused by the in-turned eye, and the weight of the hook above the bend. Every time he pulled the link up his finger, the hook would turn around and the point would go in, it wasn't possible to prevent it. I tried, facing the hook away from my finger and wriggling it this way and then trying to get the hook over my finger without it dropping round; it was impossible. I tried it with Dave's 'Swimmer' rig; sometimes it did it, but most of the time it didn't.

With all of the other rigs it had the opposite effect, turning the hook point away from the finger. If you imagine your finger to be the rim of the mouth and you imagine the bait is in the mouth and the fish is backing off, the hook is going to roll round and stick into the floor of the mouth on the way out. Get it? Now the rig has many other advantages such as the hook being high up the bait, and the point being away from the bait so it is not obscured. Of course I could be totally wrong about my theory but Savay was absolutely taken apart when I showed Martin Locke and he took it back to Savay and showed the others. Jim Martinez, one of the best anglers on Savay, took thirties of 34 lb something and 31 lb something, the first time he used it, and everyone, and I mean everyone caught more. So there you are. I certainly reaped the rewards at Fox Pool, it was singularly the most effective rig used there that year without exception. Many people have expressed their wishes for me to leave this whole section out of the book, but I haven't because as I see it putting carp on the bank is the name of the game, for everyone. I showed Kevin Maddocks the new rig with its refinements. He was convinced and I gave him the two rigs off my rods which were in my car and he used them on Duncan Kay's Mid-Northants carp fishery at Higham Ferrers, when the lake wasn't fishing well at all. The results he had doubled the whole lake's total by the other anglers fishing there at the time—proof positive; game, set and match. I have seen this rig used with a variety of hook sizes, from size 2/0's on very short hook link to 4 or 5oz fixed leads, to size 6 hooks on a conventional set up. The method I have deployed is described below:—

Apparatus

Size 6 long shank Kamasan 'Streamer' fly hook, pair of pliers, 10mm length of 1mm diameter Kevin Nash rig tube, hook link material and counterweight as described earlier.

BENT HOOK RIG

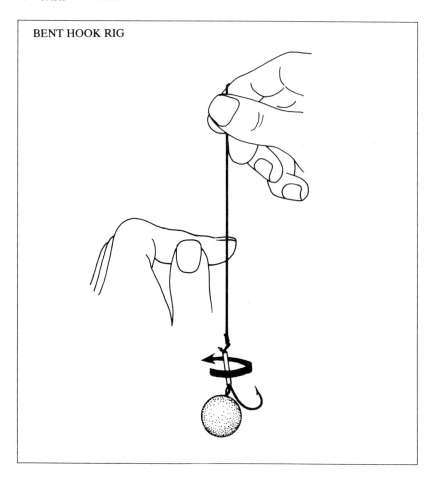

Method

Bend the hook slowly in the pliers with the eye moving towards the point and the length of straight shank being about 10 mm long; the hook point should be pointing directly at the eye. Tie the hook onto your hook link material, multi-strand or braided. Now you need a loop to tie your bait to, so either tie a loop with a half hitch to the shank, using the end left at the knot, or whip on a loop. The loop should be about 3–5 mm long to allow for anti-ejection if needed. Or what I do to form the loop is to take about six inches of 10 lb BS braid and push both ends through the 10 mm length of Kevin Nash tube. Now pull both ends down until the required loop sticks out of one end of the braid

DOUBLE BAIT, BENT HOOK RIG

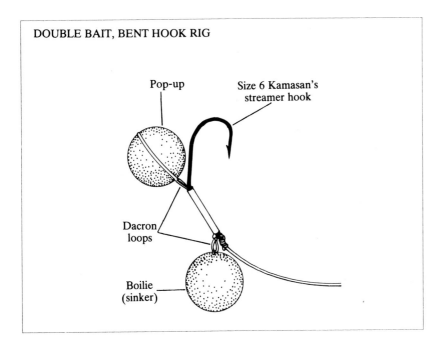

Pop-up

Size 6 Kamasan's
streamer hook

Dacron
loops

Boilie
(sinker)

close to the other end of the rig tube. This now will not pass up the tube so it keeps the loop the right size. Snip off the loose ends close to the knot, then pass the whole lot over the point of the hook, knotted end first, slide the tube down to the eye: done. A very neat method of achieving it. Now tie your pop-up on with dental floss in the traditional way. Bottom baits are equally as effective with this rig. Two other variations of the bent hook are shown in the diagrams. Both are obvious in their intention, so I won't write about them.

Multi-Strand Set Ups

I'm including these set ups not because I am using multi-strand links, which I'm not, but only because I have experimented with trying to use them; as yet I haven't found a satisfactory way of not getting tangles, not all the time, and if you are fishing in any kind of weed for instance, the whole lot ends up in a ball on many occasions. So why try and use it? We certainly can't afford to cast out twelve or more hours at a time only to reel in a ball of cotton wool. Well, the idea behind them is good as I said, they are both supple and very strong so if only we can find a way to fish them with consistent perfection they can only improve on catch rates.

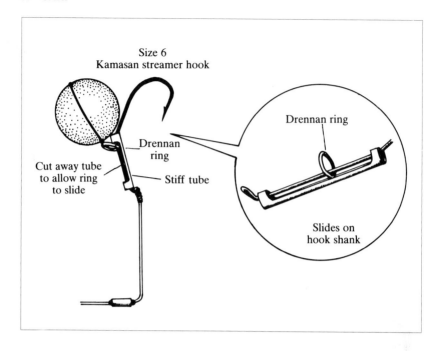

One method I have used is to tie the link every inch with a knot of PVA; this at least should get in tangle free; alternatively PVAing the link to a section of reed or stick sends it out tangle free, but by pulling back to locate clear areas, bars etc. or reeling in the whole lot can end in a real mess, and the last thing I need is a bleeding great mess, especially in the middle of the night. Fixing a stringer to the hook and sinking the tackle on a tight line usually lays the rig straight and putting the tackle in one of Rod Hutchinson's PVA tubes together with several free offerings has the same effect but to move it once it's landed can be fatal. The best method I have found is to grease the link with Vaseline. This sticks all the fibres together though and this may not be the effect you want. If you are fishing the link purely because it's limp and strong then Vaselining is okay, but if you are looking at presenting separate fibres floating in the water then it's not. So in conclusion, I must unfortunately say that I am not confident in using it, but I must also say that the concept is good. Certainly I know of many good fish taken on the stuff. Perhaps the new woven type of strand will prove to be the answer. I personally would like to see a link strand, similar in section to chain link. This is not only supple but very strong, so come on manufacturers start thinking of a fibre which under magnification has a structure similar to chain. Yet another brilliant idea that Kevin Nash will no doubt claim credit for when he thinks of it!!!

Incidentally, all of these Kevlar multi-strands in various colours, waxed and unwaxed are available on bulk spools at a fraction of the cost from most archery shops; they are used for bow strings. John Allen and Colin Martins (Longfield Drinking Team) have been using them for the past five years!

Anti-tangle Set-Ups Revised

This is my opinion again, but there's an awful lot of rubbish talked about plastic tubing and its effect on carp. I firmly believe it makes no difference to your chances of catching by using it. I've heard so many people say that carp are shy of it and are now steering clear of it on the bottom; absolute rubbish. The bottom of lakes are littered with twigs, weed and all sorts of objects, so anti-tangle tube is certainly not frightening them away. The only argument I can see against using it is if you can come up with something better than tubing; Zen Bojko may have done that.

Firstly, let me explain what items I have been messing about with to stop tangles. The Tulip Bead marketed by Leslies of Luton is certainly a useful little bead, which can be used in several different combinations; the one I prefer is shown in the diagram. It removes any corners or edges that can catch the line when the lead is in flight. Also the in-line leads introduced a couple of years ago are now becoming more widely used, either with tubing or lead-core for tangle reduction. It was Zenon who first used tubing way back when he was having incredible results on Layer Pits; who else could invent a simple but effective replacement to plastic tubing?

ZEN'S HELICOPTER RIG

Apparatus

Two large beads, one KN swivel bead, one or two DAM stops, lead and hook link.

Method

First push the rubber DAM stop(s) up the line, slide on one bead, then the swivel bead, then the other bead, then tie the lead securely on the end of the line. Pull the stop(s) down until the whole lot is close to the bomb, but not locked up solid, the swivel bead must be able to turn around freely. Now tie your hook link onto the swivel (on the swivel bead), the link can now revolve around the main line. When casting out,

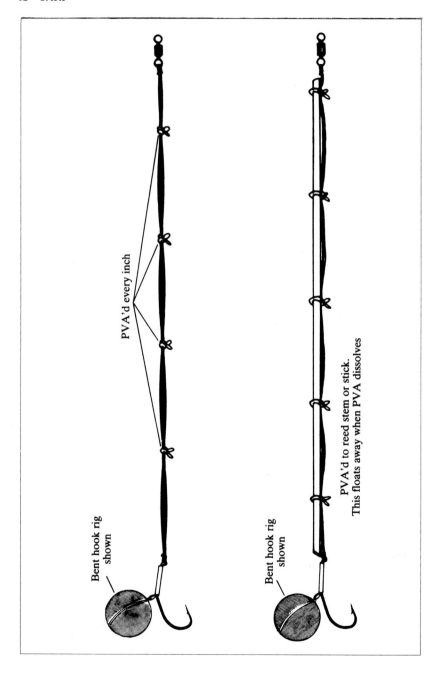

PVA'd every inch

Bent hook rig
shown

PVA'd to reed stem or stick.
This floats away when PVA dissolves

Bent hook rig
shown

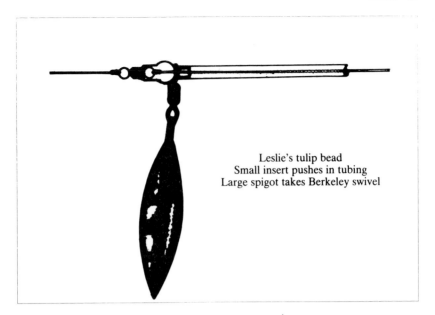

Leslie's tulip bead
Small insert pushes in tubing
Large spigot takes Berkeley swivel

the link spins like a propeller and is very efficient for anti-tangle. Multi-strand still tangles even with this rig.

So that's your lot for now, when you have used all those, I'll tell you some more. Before I go I will just say this:— when they're having it, really having it, you can catch them on any rig, but these days for 90% of the time they just ain't really having it, which is why you need such complicated rigs as these; and make no mistake an effective rig is one of, if not the most essential, parts of our armoury; good fishing.

ANTI TANGLE SET UPS REVISED

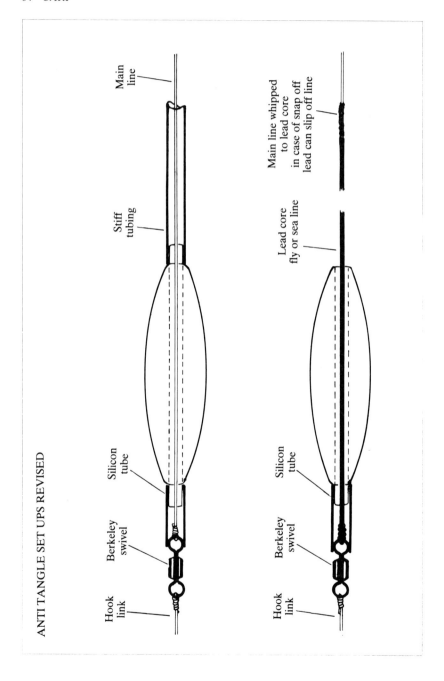

Main line

Stiff tubing

Silicon tube

Berkeley swivel

Hook link

Main line whipped to lead core in case of snap off lead can slip off line

Lead core fly or sea line

Silicon tube

Berkeley swivel

Hook link

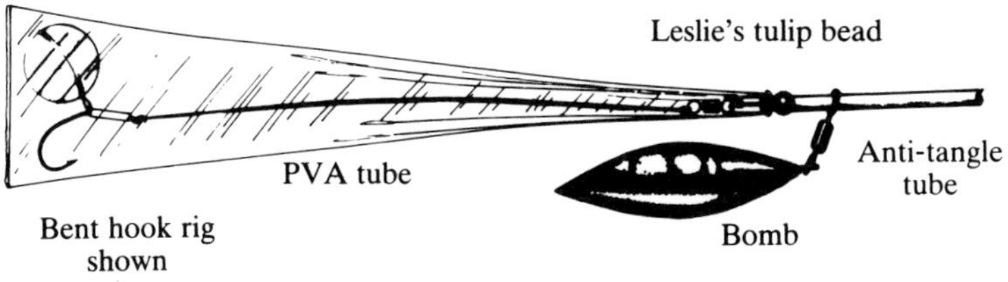

Leslie's tulip bead

PVA tube

Anti-tangle
tube

Bent hook rig
shown

Bomb

ZENON BOJKO'S HELICOPTER RIG

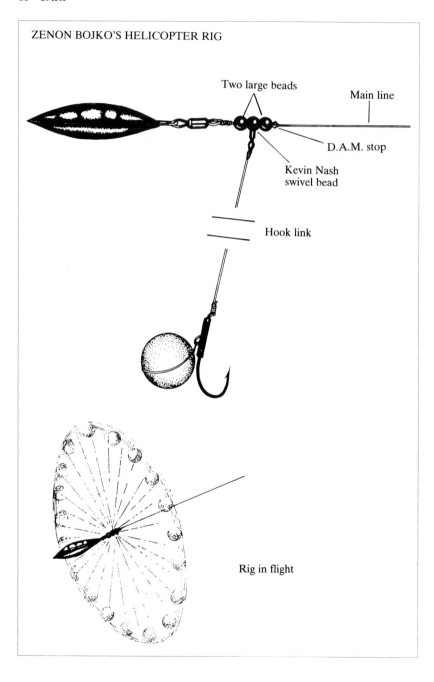

Two large beads

Main line

D.A.M. stop

Kevin Nash
swivel bead

Hook link

Rig in flight

Floater Fishing

This is not an easy one for me as my experience in this type of fishing is quite limited. I suppose if you look at my results though it all looks impressive but this I assure you is purely down to being on the right water at the right time. My expertise lies in sitting behind a pair of static rods and I would never crack myself up to be particularly good at any other type of approach. I've done most of it over the years—stalking, float fishing and surface fishing but I know there are quite a few anglers around who do far more of the sort of angling and consequently are more of authority than I. All I can do is tell you what I know, the tackle I use and a few little edges I have seen used. Perhaps you may pick up something of interest. The line should be the finest you can safely get away with, depending upon the conditions in which you intend to present your floater. For open water distance fishing where there are no snags and little if any weed, I would still be reluctant to go below an 8 lb breaking strain main line and a 6 lb breaking strain hook link, and if you are going to use any of the fashionable double strength brands I would add two pounds breaking strain to each of those. You will still be fishing a very fine line but if you are contemplating taking fish in the thirty pounds plus class I think you would be silly to go finer than that even in this open water situation.

When fishing in weedy conditions, but where it is still possible to land fish without hook and hold tactics I would be looking at using a 10 lb breaking strain main line with a 10 lb double strength hook link. Link silhouette should not be too much of a problem when fishing amongst weed, and a fair distance can still be covered with the right controller and a reasonably good quality main line.

When fishing in snags or very thick weed/lilies it really is time to consider the ethics of what could happen in these circumstances. Firstly even with the thickest of lines is it at all possible to land the fish? Secondly, if the fish takes line would it ever be possible to get it back, and thirdly and most importantly, am I sure I won't damage the fish in any way? If the answer to any of these is no, then I would give up your quest and fish somewhere else, perhaps even try and draw the fish away from the snags with loose food.

It maybe you cannot resist the temptation, it's the biggest fish in the lake, it's taking floaters like there's no tomorrows but it's right amongst the thickest snags on the lake—I know what it is like, I've been there, I've been tempted and I've failed. But that was a long time ago and a lesson was hard earned for me as I left my tackle in the fish and missed my chance. My inexperience then has left me in good stead for the later years when similar opportunities arose, and I didn't take the gamble, but managed to land it after three hours of trying to draw the fish out into open water where it was safe to land it. Last season I had a forty two pound fish taking floaters in a bush. The temptation was immense, I had a chance, but I resisted. On reflection I know I could never have landed it, and if I had have hooked it and jumped in after it or whatever I would have denied one of my mates a fish of a lifetime for he caught the fish off the bottom out in the open water the next day. Fate has a strange way of kicking you in the conkers some days! I've mentioned 'double strength' lines, and I like to use them as hook links for most of my floater fishing because they are so thin and as fish see all things floating on the surface as a silhouette against the sky, the thinner the line the better.

Controllers, fixed or running? Several years ago I had great success using a fixed polyball anchored floater rig which works in the same way as the bolt rig. A large polystyrene ball is permanently fixed on the line about twelve inches from the hook and when the fish takes the floater it pulls into the polyball much the same as a fish pulling in to a fixed lead, the hook is pulled home and the polyball retains a constant pressure on the hook hold as the fish runs. It all sounds great but unless the fish are throwing all caution to the wind they will not take the bait confidently enough to hook themselves, which is what I found at Longfield. So I prefer to use a running controller for most of my fishing and rely on chemically sharpened hooks and the resistance of the line to do my initial pricking with the hook point.

On to which type of controller and there really is a huge variety to choose from, so I'll list a few with their relative plusses and minuses.

Bubble Float: I spent several seasons using these and used to swear by them. The only advantage I can see is that fish seem to feed confidently close to them, which I think is because there is not much of the float under water and what is under water is clear. Unfortunately they don't cast well, they land with an almighty splash if you have loaded them with water, and they are difficult to cast accurately.

Film Canister: Something I see used quite a bit on some waters. I cannot see one good reason to use them with so many better alternatives available.

Candle: A cheap and easy way to make a controller which is both accurate to cast, lands fairly well and sits nicely in the water. Simply expose enough wick to tie a Berkeley swivel on and thread it onto your line.

Mixer Fixer: This is a commercially made float come bait dropper which although I have never seen anyone using one does look pretty good. The float is hollow and can be loaded with mixers which are held in place by a polyball. When the float is cast out the polyball rises, releasing the mixers.

Vaned Drifting Float: This type of float was made famous by that brilliant pike angler Eddie Turner. The principle of its use is that a smallish float with a large plastic vane can be placed into the wind so that the wind drifts the float out into the middle of the lake. Pike anglers use deadbaits, we used mixers and the distance which can be covered is far greater than you could ever cast. This method can be deadly when the fish are taking at range, and I have seen excellent results achieved with this set up. It's quite amazing to see the float suddenly disappear at 150 yards plus range.

Beachcaster Rig: This particular rig has been well documented in the past and I've no desire to go all through it again. Providing all conditions are right I suppose it could be quite effective. I personally do not like it and the type of lakes I've been fishing recently, deep and weedy, don't lend themselves to this rig.

Weighted Controller: I've deliberately left this one until last because it is my favourite and the type of float I use for 95% of my floater fishing. In particular the brass weighted balsa controllers marketed by Kevin Nash are absolutely brilliant, they cast to the horizon, land like a feather and are very accurate. If you haven't tried them give them a go. I cannot fault them. There are other similar designs on the market including a clear bodied variety but they just don't have the casting ability.

Well that just about covers controllers so I will write a bit about rigs although I haven't really experimented to any great extent on the top. This could well be the one area where great advances will be made in the next few years and I do know that a couple of my friends are already experimenting with a 'critically balanced' surface rig which when sucked offers almost no resistance and shoots straight to the throat teeth giving the fish little chance of inspecting the bait—but that's another story. The two rigs I have been using for the past couple of years has either been a straight 'through the eye' type rig, using a small and extremely sharp hook such as the Kamasan chemically sharpened, or the 'bent hook' used with two mixers, one tied conventionally on the bend of the hook and the other sticking out of the back of the eye. An example of this type of rig can be seen in the rig chapter. These two rigs have basically suited all my requirements for surface fishing although, as I said, I'm sure there is room for improvement in this area.

Bait is a matter of personal preference: Chum Mixers, Munchies, Go-Cat, Omega or even a home made floater mix can all be very effective. Mixers have always been my personal favourite, and one little edge that I do is to get a household plant sprayer, you know the sort of thing I mean, like a window cleaning spray, and fill it with either minamino or liquid liver, or bulk oils or better still one of the bait soaks such as the marine spice emulsions and spray your mixers, which will form an attractive flavour slick on the surface, a bit like rubby dubby attracting sharks, and the results can be quite devastating on waters that have even been heavily fished with Mixers before.

If you haven't surface fished before give it a go, the results can be very rewarding, sometimes when fish will have nothing off the bottom a few Mixers can turn them into a feeding frenzy. Floater fishing is something I intend to investigate sometime over the next few seasons, though my results this year have been conclusive enough. In one three morning session I took fish at 37.12, 34.12, 31.08 all off the top, and on a water that was quite definitely the hardest lake I've ever fished.

Guidelines

Before I go on to give you a few examples of when plumbing, location and baiting paid off in style let us quickly re-cap on some of the bench marks we should try to observe when considering a season in pursuit of known big carp.

1 Close Season Preparation

Choose at least two big fish to go for so that if one gets caught by someone else you have a standby fish to fall back on. Spend as much time in the close season on the water as you can, plumbing etc. will be invaluable once the season arrives.

2 Start of the Season

If you intend to do a session at the start of the season, get installed on the water with as much time to spare as you can, so that any plumbing, baiting or general disturbance on the bank is all done well before the off, thus giving the swim chance to settle down and fish to become confident again.

3 Mid-Season

Although the start of the season can be quite explosive at times due to the rest period the carp have received, once the season gets under way, and prior to Autumn weight gain, the fishing may well slow down. This time of the season is generally the warmest and in my experience often the most unproductive. Try some floater fishing on these hot calm summer days (or nights)! Don't overdo the baiting if it looks as if feeding has slowed down. Try to be on the water for dawn if you only intend to do a single days fishing; this is often most productive at this time of the day.

4 Autumn (September–November)

Prime time! In my experience this is often the most productive time of the season. The fish will be intent on building up their body weights to carry them through the colder months and in case of hardship. This explains why many of the fish you catch at this time will be at their best weights around the 38–36lb mark in July and could now give you the chance to break the forty barrier, with a bit of luck. This is also the time of year that I use the most bait. I don't think you can overdo boilies or particles at this time of year, if the fish are on the bait.

5 Mild Winter

By mild winter I'm really talking about winters like the past two seasons; hardly any freeze up and only a few really heavy frosts. This, too, can be an exciting time of the year. Much of the pressure is often gone from the water but the fish will still be feeding if only for shorter periods. This is perhaps my favourite time of the season—no 'mossies'!

6 Hard Winter or Freeze Up

Now we've got problems, and it will usually take a settled period of warmer weather of at least two weeks before the fish will respond again. I do know of some quite outstanding catches in the coldest of weathers, so it's always possible, but as a general guide these are the hardest times to catch fish. On the plus side you may catch one in the snow. These are only rough outlines, not gospel, so don't quote me on any, but in my experience these bench marks follow the same routine every season.

Putting it into Practice

This is quite obviously not a book of stories, as were my two previous publications. This is a technical reference book, as it was conceived to be, but it's all very well me saying do this and do that but unless you can actually see some of these things I have written about being put into practice the whole lot falls a bit flat. Theory is great but results are what count. So what I'd like to do is give you three examples of where location, watercraft, baiting and a result all come together in extremely different circumstances, floater fishing, summer fishing and winter fishing. By giving you these three examples you can see how each little thing is used in its own way and the theory part of it becomes much more than that.

Floater Fishing Summer 1989

My choice of water was to be the Leisure Sport venue at Staines, known as Longfield, or, more lately, Fox Pool. The reasons I chose to fish here were several: firstly, it had been an ambition of mine for many years to catch a really big fish off the top and going by previous years this was possible in the right conditions. Secondly I had free time mid-week when I knew the lake would be under a lot less pressure than the weekend. Thirdly it was hot, almost flat calm and none of the thirties had been caught from the water so far this season. So this was it, everything had fallen into place nicely and I had four free days in which to catch a big surface mirror.

Tackle was pretty basic, but it had to be capable of distances up to ninety yards. So, thirteen foot extreme range Tricast, Shimano 4.5, ten pound Maxima main line, ten pounds Drennan Double Strength hook link, Kevin Nash long range controller, and a size six Kamasan (chemically sharpened) to finish it off.

Bait, Pedigree Chum Mixers, lightly sprayed with Obsession Tandoori bait soak.

I arrived at the lake at around nine in the morning. I didn't need much tackle, as I wanted to be mobile. Location was the first priority, but location with one other factor in mind, the wind. The wind was almost non-existent but what wind there was I needed off my back if possible so that all the free Mixers would drift out into the lake. It's not always possible to get that combination but if I can I always have the wind over my shoulder, that way you should only need a catapult to put the feed out, rather than noisy spodding with a bait dropper.

A decent pair of sunglasses is essential when trying to locate fish under these conditions and a reasonable pair of shoes which will enable you to climb any available look-out trees if you are permitted to do so under the fishery rules. In other words if you need waders to fish make sure you have a pair of trainers with you just in case.

I made my way slowly around the lake, looking hard into the snag trees which line the bank in one corner of the pool. Nothing to be seen, but the sun was full up and I would expect the fish to be out in the lake enjoying it. I saw two carp in the first swim I came to along the bank with what little wind there was came from behind me. I carried along that bank until I came to a large open swin half way along. This particular swim is ideal for surface or bottom fishing in that you can command a great deal of the lake from this position. Ideally the swim also has a forty foot climbing tree, ten yards down the bank so I was quickly up that with the Polaroids to see if any fish were in the area. I could see at least three carp at range and another two close in, not doing much, just lazing about in the sun; down the tree with stealth and quietly into the swim. I catapulted several pouchfuls of Mixers out into the edge of the wind and began to set up my rod. Some time elapsed before two fish began to take interest in the loose feed. A quick look up the tree again gave away their identities, 'Shoulders' and 'Parrot', both around the 35lb mark. I did panic a bit at this time and ruined this first chance of the day but without going in to the things I did wrong I did learn some important lessons. Firstly cast the float as infrequently as possible—the less disturbance the better. I know this sounds obvious but it's very tempting to cast at every taking fish instead of just leaving the float where it is, baiting to it, and waiting for them to come to you, which they will if only you can be patient. Secondly, try not to bait too heavily—little and often is far better as you can lose your fish as they follow the Mixer drift, either out of range or worse still out in front of someone else, who can easily cash in on all your hard work with a simple flick in the right direction.

So as I said I did mess up my first chance but all was not lost as a while later after keeping a steady feed line snaking out into the lake another fish began to show interest at the ninety yard mark. With the float I had chosen I was able to reach this fish and the result was a superb mirror of 31lb 12oz. This was not the end of the action and over the next two days, following the same basic procedures I took fish of 34 lb 12 oz and 37 lb 8 oz—an incredible catch by any standards and one which would be hard to match. However, on the right water and with the right conditions, who knows what can be achieved?

Winter Fishing (Bottom) 1986

I had quite a few eventful winter trips to choose from but in the end I've settled for one particular session on the Copse lake at Yateley, a superb little water owned by Leisure Sport Angling, in Surrey. It was a totally new water to us when we began fishing it just after Christmas. Being small, only a couple of acres, the five of us that chose to tackle it had an immediate advantage in that if we spread ourselves around someone was almost bound to find the fish, and being winter the fish were probably shoaled up tight, so whoever dropped right would give the rest of us the chance to get in on the action.

It was Dave Whibley who chose right on our first session on the water. Dave dropped in the centre of the large open expanse of water at one end, next to a string of small islands. He took a mirror of 26 lb that session, but more importantly he had given us both confidence and a shove in the right direction.

Next session I moved to his right, at the end of the line of islands but still facing the open expanse of water. Being first on the lake this weekend it gave me a good opportunity to plumb the water in front. The first thing I did was to cast a marker float from Dave's swim to where he caught the fish. Then I went back to my swim and pinpointed the area. I didn't want to encroach on his spot when he arrived but I wanted to know what was out there and why, if possible, he had caught.

Dave had taken his fish between two large dead weed beds, and it was my opinion that the fish were lying up in this weed. The leeches that the 26 was carrying indicated that it had been lying dormant. I then cast all around the open area until I found a very similar feature, a long gulley between two large beds of dead weed about thirty feet to the right of Dave's spot. That will do for me, I thought. Accurate casting is essential on these small weedy lakes: a foot in the wrong spot is as good as a mile. I had found enough room for two baits and put in about thirty free baits in the area. The others arrived and carried out similar exercises, and soon we were all cast out to holes in the weed beds.

All quiet the first night, but I did put a few more baits out at first light just in case the ducks had eaten the first lot. It was around mid-day when the take came—my first Yateley carp. A fish known as 'Crinkle Tail', which weighed 30 lb 4 oz. So—location, accurate casting and baiting; the bait, incidentally, was spice bird seed: once the combination comes together the right result can be achieved.

Summer Fishing (Bottom) June 1989

I am going to use Poplars Lake in Kent as my example for this, not because the fish were particularly large, but because three of us caught at different times on this session, which goes to prove one thing, we were all doing it right; as soon as the fish were with us, one of us caught, and so on. The lake we were fishing was about twelve acres in size, deep, weedy and the fish were well clued up. The stock was mainly twenties but there are a couple of low thirties as well.

We fished the lake in a triangle formation, Dave Whibley, Phil Harper and I, south, east and west banks, one of each. We all spent about six hours plumbing the area thoroughly before the season opened, and soon discovered quite a large clear area at distance. This clear area seemed ideal as you have a large bank of weed along which the fish could move easily.

Although we were all using slightly different flavourings the base mix was the same, bird seed with HNV pop-ups fished over the top on the same flavour. Dave was on the fish just before the start of the season but by the time we could cast out, they had moved on the wind and he had to wait a full day before they returned once again out in front of him, tightly shoaled up. Dave took fish of 20lb 8oz and 21lb during the next two days. All the other swims were quiet, but Phil and I kept baiting hard. We knew the fish would move again because of the pressure Dave was putting on them and we weren't wrong.

It was I that received the next action and took two more fish 25lb 4oz and 24lb 4oz in a one hour hot period as the fish moved along my bank. I would estimate that at the time the shoal arrived I had upward of three thousand baits in my swim—it didn't stop them, and I doubt that were many baits left out there when they had all departed.

They moved on the wind out in front of Phil, and he took fish of 23lb 8oz and 22lb 8oz the next day. Six fish, all over twenty, from a hard lake, good going, that's for sure. So follow the guide lines:— location, loose feed, plumbing and presentation. It's all in the book; be lucky.

Mild February conditions produced this Springwood mid-twenty.

Please remember — litter loses fishing

So What Have We Learnt?

1 Study the weeklies—they can be invaluable.
2 Buy my books!
3 Choose at least two big fish to go after.
4 Try to keep in touch with what is going on in your absence.
5 It may be advantageous to fish closely with others.
6 Get confidence in baits and rigs before you start on hard waters.
7 Try to get background information on the waters you are going to.
8 Talk to people.
9 Don't be a prat on a new water and upset everyone.
10 Plumb as much as you can.
11 Write down everything that happens while you are there.
12 Don't expect instant success; be patient.
13 Be very careful with anything you catch, someone else will want to catch it in just as good condition next time.
14 Put out freebies with the head of fish in mind.
15 Don't overbait in winter.
16 Be conservation minded and don't overdo flavour levels etc.
17 If someone is forthcoming with information be just as forthcoming to him.
18 If the pressure gets to you have a break. An hour in the pub or even a session on an easy lake can work wonders.
19 Try to be considerate to other anglers on the water—some of them may have been there a long time.
20 When success comes, as I'm sure it will, keep your head and you will continue to be as successful.

Well, that's about it, lads; the concise pocket book of big carp fishing. It's always been my intent to enjoy my fishing to the full and never to let it get too serious. On the other hand I have respect for the serious amongst you; fishing means different things to different people.

For me its always been a release from the pressures of work and therefore I try not to let pressure get involved in my fishing. Sometimes it's hard especially if I'm struggling and someone close to me is having it easy. What you have got to remember is that you just won't catch them all, not with the class of angler coming up through the ranks.

So at the end of the day regardless of whether or not we have caught or not we should always be able to say, 'It was a great session, I've enjoyed it'. If you can say that even when you are blanking you will be even more pleased when success comes your way. Perhaps I'll meet some of you on my travels this season; I like a chat and I like a pint even better! We are all out there to catch them so let's just make sure we don't lose sight of why we do it—for pleasure.

Go out and whack 'em.
'Rob'